RECOLLECTIONS
OF A
HITHERTO TRUTHFUL MAN

MONGREL EMPIRE PRESS
NORMAN, OKLAHOMA, UNITED STATES OF AMERICA

Norman, Oklahoma 2013

FIRST EDITION, 2013

Recollections of a Hitherto Truthful Man:
Personal / Historical Essays

© 2013 by Davis D. Joyce

ISBN 978-0-9851337-6-4

Cover Image:
At Common Ground Farm, Kiamichi Mountains,
SE Oklahoma
© Ashley Porton 2013

Author Photo:
© Laura Stanfill, 2013

Mongrel Empire Press
Norman, OK

Online catalogue: www.mongrelempire.org

ꜣ

Book Design: Mongrel Empire Press using iWork Pages

To my grandchildren
Rosina, Manny, Gabby Marie, and Charly

And in memory of Howard Zinn

RECOLLECTIONS
OF A
HITHERTO TRUTHFUL MAN

Personal / Historical Essays

Davis D. Joyce

TABLE OF CONTENTS

Acknowledgments

First and foremost, I acknowledge my wife, Carole, the love of my life—and my first editor on all of my books for 35 years now!

I wish also to acknowledge Jeanetta Calhoun Mish. I have long respected her work, both as a poet and a publisher. She found a place for me and my book at her Mongrel Empire Press after a long and painful experience with another publisher. Thank you, Jeanetta.

Frank Elwell and Shelly Borgstrom of Rogers State University deserve a vigorous thank you for helping me with "computer problems;" like just about anyone who knows me, they know that, for me, computers *are* a problem.

My dedication to my grandchildren and the memory of Howard Zinn perhaps speaks for itself, but allow me to add just two brief comments. I have dedicated books over the years to Carole, my Mom and Dad, my brother and his family (and in memory of our sister), my children, and my step-children; the dedication of this one to my grandchildren speaks to my realization, which has grown as I have aged, that there is indeed nothing more important than family. And the dedication to the memory of Howard Zinn is also important to me. If you read much of this book, you will see what a powerful influence he exercised on me.

Kathy Henslee, a school teacher in Antlers, Oklahoma, and a friend of mine through our daughter, Elizabeth Barlow, read the entire manuscript for me. And Rachel Jackson read parts of it as well. Rachel is a former student and now a good friend. It gives me hope that she and her *Red Flag Press* and *Oklahoma*

Revelator will carry on some of the important values in Oklahoma for many years to come.

Finally, I should acknowledge *The Key*, a publication of the South Sebastian County [Arkansas] Historical Society, Historians Against the War, the *East Central University Research Journal*, *The Oklahoma Revelator*, and the *Red Dirt Anthology* for allowing me to reprint items here which originally appeared in their pages.

Davis D. Joyce
Lake Spavinaw, Oklahoma
October 1, 2013

Foreword

The 1960s had a profound and very sweeping effect upon American life and culture. The energy of American youth that fueled progressive reforms during that period spurred historic changes in areas such as civil rights, women's rights, the environment, and a number of social net programs. In short, the sixties represented a watershed era in American history. However, the successful fight to abolish long standing antiquated institutional structures eventually created a conservative backlash that consistently struggled to slow, if not completely reverse, the pace of reform.

Colleges and universities did not—could not—remain immune to the powerful sweep of change that characterized America during the sixties. Social and political activism affected, and was affected by, the youthful students and many of their professors. Davis Joyce entered graduate school at the University of Oklahoma just as the civil rights movement had begun to move forcefully ahead but had not nearly approached its zenith. And it would be civil rights and America's involvement in the Vietnam War that would profoundly influence his career as an important scholar, teacher, and activist. Undoubtedly, his attraction to the anti-Vietnam War movement had much to do with his intellectual acquaintance with the works and activities of anti-war activist and scholar, Howard Zinn. Much later, Joyce chose to write a well-received biography of this man who made such an indelible imprint upon the war protest movement, but in the process excited the hatred of more than one politician and pro-war advocate.

The engaging and thought provoking essays here reveal the powerful impact that Zinn had upon Joyce. Yet, what the reader sees in those articles, or is reasonably able to deduce, is an earlier appreciation of Joyce for "truth-telling" and a response to negative elements within American society that pre-dated his familiarity with Zinn. Historians' ideas about events often take place over time and rarely represent revolutionary visions that suddenly appear. An event that took place in Joyce's life nearly two years before he became acquainted with Zinn's ideas on Vietnam or civil rights illustrates the point about the shaping of ideas. In 1965, a hate-filled citizen of Selma, Alabama, clubbed to death a minister named James Reeb who had gone South to participate in the Selma to Montgomery March for voting rights. Students at the University of Oklahoma held a memorial service for Reeb as a small group of racially conservative students looked on in protest, one of whom aggressively waved a small confederate flag. Davis Joyce attended that celebration of Reverend Reeb's life; and the fact that he chose to do that with the writer of this foreword—an African-American native of Mississippi—said much about influences upon him before he came to the University at Norman. Perhaps the essay in this book on his "Sebastian County Mother" helps to explain much about his attitude. So, hardly did Zinn have to work overtime to convince Joyce about the direction of his intellectual life, or how the teaching of history could, and often did, have some direct bearing upon social thought and practical behavior.

Joyce has assembled essays that inform us of his personal views of history, but importantly they also prompt us to think seriously about many of the challenges in contemporary American society. What we have before us does not represent the idle musings of an aging scholar faced with some kind of mid-life crisis! Nowhere is truth telling and honest thought revealed more clearly than in Joyce's comments on teaching and scholarship. Much like Zinn, Joyce snatches the cover off the scholarly myth of "objectivity" in history. For too long, he contends, teachers, especially in the social sciences, have been neither honest nor objective. Often so-called objectivity has amounted to nothing more than fiction that sustained a status quo, hid prejudices or masked ideology. However, Joyce's beliefs do not give license to lies, misrepresentation of events, or shoddy scholarship. What Joyce cautions against is intellectual deception and an unyielding dogmatism that says "I've got it right and nothing else really counts." Significantly, he calls for transparency, notably in what people teach, write or advocate.

This work skillfully examines several notable themes, but perhaps none protrudes as much or with such captivating power as that of place and its possible influences upon us. In his perceptive essay "Willie Morris' *North Toward Home* . . ." Joyce compares his Arkansas/New Mexico/Oklahoma experiences with those of writer Willie Lee Morris, a Mississippian, who moved to Texas and then to New York City. Readers will again appreciate the warmth, comfort, and dynamics of regional culture, and what it means to have that culture clash head-on with more forceful national trends. Historians who have closely examined place will have even greater reason to laud Joyce's efforts. In the past scholars have rightly focused sharply upon the positive attractions of place. In Joyce's commentary, he enables the reader to comprehend how negative features of a culture can actually promote reform, albeit subtle, among a region's natives.

We have in Davis Joyce's essay a remarkably honest rendition of a philosophy grounded in respect for other people and an appreciation for honest scholarship that is not a blind slave to ideology or self-interest. His reflections go beyond intellectual abstractions; and his comments will resonate among those persons who understand the meaning of folk life, small town culture, and the existence of the "average" American.

Among many readers, the volume will inspire critical reflection about history, human experience, and the nature of contemporary American democracy. The question that seems to shout out at us persistently is "what will we do to determine the shape of democracy in the years to come?" And what seems to underlie that question is one that exists at the very core of our national life: "will we passively regard our Constitution as a static political instrument, as many people insist, or will we regard it as a living document flexible enough to foster the general welfare of all the people?" Translated into practical political terms, the answer to those questions may determine our fate and whether we fulfill the hopes of the founding fathers. Joyce's work reflects a progressive or reform outlook that has been a central feature in American life for many years. With characteristic frankness, he unveils notable tensions within our culture that call for reasoned debate, tolerance, and civility in our personal relationships and politics as our country struggles to fashion policies that serve the general welfare of all its people, not just the privileged few among us. If I read Joyce correctly or understand his distinguished scholarly career of nearly four decades, I hear a clarion call for us to rekindle a spirit of national unity that the founding fathers envisioned so that America does not falter in its continuing quest for the good life.

Jimmie Lewis Franklin
Professor of History, Emeritus
Vanderbilt University

Jimmie Lewis Franklin took his Ph. D. in American history in 1968 at the University of Oklahoma. A student of the state's past, he has written three well-received books on Oklahoma. Franklin was also the 1993 president of the Southern Historical Association. He is now Professor Emeritus at Vanderbilt University.

Introduction

Since retiring from full-time teaching in 2002, I have found, without planning it, that my writing has taken a turn toward the personal. I wrote a brief tribute to my Mother, focusing on life's lessons I feel I learned from her. Then I wrote an essay entitled "War, Howard Zinn, and Me," which I presented at the 2008 meeting of the national organization Historians Against the War. Next came an essay on "Common Ground Farm and Oklahoma Character." Common Ground is the intentional community (think "commune," as it would have been called in the 1960s) in southeastern Oklahoma where our daughter lives—and to show how important a place it is to me, I should note that my ashes will be spread there one of these days. This one was presented at the 2007 Red Dirt Book Festival in Shawnee, Oklahoma, the theme of which was "Oklahoma Character." Then I had the uncontrollable urge to write a piece, I truly had no idea for what purpose, entitled "Race, the Rebel Flag, and My Home Town: A Rant." I shared it with only a couple of friends, both of whom suggested I should write a book pursuing further the personal thrust of my recent writings. My wife, Carole, encouraged me in this direction also. I thought of an autobiography, a memoir, even a novel. But none of these felt right to me. I discussed all this with Frank Elwell, a sociologist friend of mine, the Dean of Liberal Arts at Rogers State University in Claremore, Oklahoma, who made the breakthrough for me: "Why not make it a collection of personal essays?" That immediately felt right, and it is essentially what you get here.

The title of this book is borrowed from Edward Channing; the approach is more akin to that of Howard Zinn.

My first book, published in 1974, was on the life and writings of late 19th/early 20th-century Harvard historian Edward Channing, best known for his six-volume *History of the United States*, the sixth volume of which, on the Civil War era, won the Pulitzer Prize for 1925.[1] Late in his life, Channing started work on a memoir. He never finished it, and so it was never published, except in a private printing of a limited run of numbered copies after his death in 1931. He called it "Recollections of a Hitherto Truthful Man." I always thought that was funny, yet quite insightful as well. It seemed to me he was trying to say, essentially: "Look, I'm a historian, and I've always tried to tell the truth in my work, but be aware that I'm now an old man, and you should perhaps take what I say with a grain of salt." Have you ever noticed that the memories of old folks, even those who experienced the same things, don't always match up?

Many years later, in 2003, I published a study of the life and writings of radical activist and historian Howard Zinn.[2] Zinn was involved prominently in the civil rights movement and the anti-Vietnam War movement, but is best known as the author of the best-selling 1980 book, *A People's History of the United States*. For those unfamiliar with the idea of "people's history," it might help to note that it's sometimes called "history from the bottom up." Have you ever noticed how much traditional history, without ever saying so, was written "from the top down"? In other words, there was lots of information about Presidents, kings, queens, generals, rich people, but very little about common folks. People's history in part addresses that problem. Zinn, in that sense, was a part of the "new social history" of the 1960s and after. Further, it might help to note that people's history, as done by Zinn and others, is frequently "history from the outside in" as well. That is to say, Zinn's heros and heroines are the men and women who worked for change, who worked for peace and justice, such as the abolitionists, women's rights advocates, and anti-war activists.

Howard Zinn had a profound impact on me over the years, both personally and professionally—though one of the things he taught me is that we tend to separate the two too much! As a young assistant professor of history at the University of Tulsa in the 1960s, I was certainly beginning to have my doubts about what we were doing in Vietnam, and even more doubts about whether our government was telling us the truth about it. But having been born in 1940, and having grown up in a family with two uncles who served in the military in World War II and a father who didn't only because he couldn't, I was conditioned to think that if your country went to war, you simply supported it, no questions asked. So I was even feeling a little guilty about the doubts I was having. Reading Howard Zinn's 1967 book, *Vietnam: The Logic of Withdrawal*, helped me get over that, and I was soon actively involved in the anti-war movement myself. Later, Zinn's approach to history in general, in books like *The Politics of History* as well as *A People's History of the United States*, influenced my teaching and my research and writing as a historian; for example, I put together over the years two Zinn-influenced collections of essays on Oklahoma history.[3]

So, again, we have here Channing's title, but a Zinnian approach. What do I mean by the sub-title, "Personal/Historical Essays"? Partly, it means that I'm telling about history that I was involved in, for example the civil rights movement and the anti-Vietnam War movement. (I like to think that I "coined" the term "personal/historical essays" in my first Oklahoma history book as an effort to describe work that was certainly part of history, involved change over time, etc., but that the person writing it was deeply involved in it; some of the people I recruited to write such essays were not professional historians at all. If "common folks" are going to be *in* history, shouldn't they be empowered to *tell* their stories as well?) But even when I'm writing here about history that I certainly was not involved in, such as the material in Will Durant's *The Story of Civilization*, it's still personal in that I feel deeply connected to that material, and write about it accordingly.

Another way of saying essentially the same thing, perhaps, is that the traditional notion of historical "objectivity" is simply not relevant here. Zinn helped me understand that as well. Objectivity, he insisted, is neither possible nor desirable. Human nature being what it is, each of us is going to bring a point of view to the subject. And what if one could accomplish total objectivity, "just the facts"? Wouldn't that be history that would tend to prop up the status quo, and therefore be about as "political" as history could possibly be? Better, thought Zinn, and I agree, to be open and honest and up front about your biases to the greatest extent possible, and then proceed to write the best history you can write. There's nothing here that says you shouldn't get your facts straight; obviously, you should. And there's nothing here that says you have the right to mess with the sources, to twist them and make things up; obviously, you don't. Personal/historical essays. That description hopefully ties together the various parts of this volume which at a glance might appear quite diverse indeed.

Though not formally divided into three parts, the twelve chapters seem to me to flow from this personal/historical kind of essay to some that focus more on teaching to some that focus more on Oklahoma—but note that my personal attachment to teaching and to Oklahoma is deep! So I hope all of them qualify as "personal/historical essays."

1 Davis D. Joyce, *Edward Channing and the Great Work* (The Hague, Netherlands: Martinus Nijhoff, 1974).

2 Davis D. Joyce, *Howard Zinn: A Radical American Vision* (Amherst, New York: Prometheus Books, 2003).

3 *"An Oklahoma I Had Never Seen Before:" Alternative Views of Oklahoma History* (Norman: University of Oklahoma Press, 1994); and *Alternative Oklahoma: Contrarian Views of the Sooner State* (Norman: University of Oklahoma Press, 2007).

CHAPTER 1

Some Wisdom from My Sebastian County Mother

This essay originally appeared in *The Key*, a publication of the South Sebastian County [Arkansas] Historical Society (Vol. 40, 2007). I should note that my Mother died on July 21, 2008. It makes me very proud that she liked this piece a lot, kept the issue of *The Key* that included it by the side of her bed until the day she died, showing it to anyone who hadn't seen it.

☮

I thought about calling this little essay "The Wisdom of My Sebastian County Mother," but that's too pretentious. I don't have it all yet; I'm still learning.

Many years ago, my brother's wife was in a conversation with a group of her friends, all young married women. The topic: mothers-in-law. Not surprisingly, some horror stories were coming out. My brother's wife remembers that at some point her friends began to realize she hadn't contributed anything to the conversation, and attention seemed to turn to her. She shrugged, and said, "I don't really have anything to say. My mother-in-law's a saint!"

Recently, a nephew of mine referred to my Mother as "the most saintly lady I know."

I love my Mother very much. That's part of the point here. But she's no saint. Indeed, one of the things she's taught me is that none of us are. I know quite a few "Arkansas boys" who would say their Mother was the best a guy could possibly have had. The difference? With me, it's really true! And I still have her at this point in my life, when I'm 67 and she's 93—what a blessing!

"Wisdom," you see—according to a 1942 *Webster's New Illustrated Dictionary* Mama gave me when I was a little boy—means "sagacity, prudence, good judgment; great learning." Yes, *that* is what I have learned, am still learning, from my Mother. But have you ever noticed how a dictionary definition forces you to look up other words? What, exactly, I wondered, is sagacity? Well, according to my 1942 dictionary (which still has my name in the front as "Davie Joyce, Greenwood, Arkansas, Route 1"—Davie was my little boy name), it means "quick, keen judgment," the "ability to see promptly what should be done in a difficult situation." And prudence? That's "wisdom in practical affairs." Full circle, see? And finally, "great learning." That doesn't have to be "book learning." I can remember my Dad telling me more than once, "Son, you've got a lot of book learning, but you don't have much common sense." Part of the point here is that Mom has both. Much of her wisdom is *folk* wisdom, coming from life experience rather than books. When she graduated from Greenwood High School in 1932, as valedictorian of her class (earlier, she had also been Homecoming Queen, so wisdom wasn't the only thing she had going for her!), she "should" have gone to college. But in Depression-era Arkansas, for a girl, that just wasn't an option. Still, her knowledge, ability—her wisdom — was recognized by the school system, so that she actually served as a substitute teacher for some years without ever having any college education. (By the way, Mom graduated one night, got married to Dad the next—and, my brother and I like to tease her, started to turn grey the next!)

To share with you a bit of the wisdom I feel like I've acquired from Mama, let me start with the general and move to a couple of specifics. By "the general," I mean *attitude* toward life, how to live your life, how, among other things, to make the best out of difficult circumstances. Daddy died eighteen years ago. He and Mom had been married well over fifty years. I worried that Mom might become one of those many widows (it happens to widowers, as well) who could not adjust, and she did go through a difficult period. But she made a decision to move in with a nephew and his family (a decision I opposed, not having enough wisdom yet to see what a good move that was!), and for over a decade functioned as a vital part of that family unit. She always assured me that she would know when it was time to make a change in her living arrangements, and about seven years ago, after she began to suffer from recurring bouts of congestive heart failure, she informed all of us it was time for a change, and moved into an assisted living center, then about three years ago a nursing home. (One of the many blessings with Mama is that her mind has remained clear, so she has been able to make those decisions for herself.) She thrived living with my nephew. She thrived living in the assisted living center. She has thrived living in the nursing home. Making the best out of changing, sometimes difficult situations. Wisdom.

Have you ever visited a nursing home? Let's be honest: You'll see lots of folks who are either out of it, or living in negativity. Mama, on the other hand, enjoys life. Indeed, she informed me recently that she didn't have much patience with people who were always, in her words, "throwing a pity party." (Patience may be a virtue Mom still needs to work on; I said she wasn't a saint, remember?) The point was clear. *She* could dwell on the negative. God knows there has been plenty. She lost her husband, mother, and daughter, for example. And all in the month of May! But, typical of her ability to find the positive anywhere, she tries to focus on the fact that May is the month of my wife's birthday, so that she has something pleasant to associate with it! And there's more of the negativity. Mom hasn't been able to walk, for example, for several years now, and lives a tenuous existence with the congestive heart failure, going from one hospitalization to the other recently, it seems. But if you visit her, that's not what you think about. You think what a pleasant person she is to visit with! What is that? I'm not uncomfortable calling it wisdom. I don't know if I even *want* to live to be 93 (though Mom tells me there's one group of people who do: those who are 92!), but if I do, I hope I can use my Arkansas Mother as an inspiration and role model!

It's wisdom, I suggest, that helps Mama continue to have the positive attitude she does. But it's also faith. Once, not long ago, I asked her how she does it, how she holds onto a positive attitude toward life when so many around her in her situation seem to have turned so negative (or be throwing a pity party!). Her first answer was, "My faith." She's a lifelong, devout Southern Baptist. But careful—if you're starting, as you read that, to fall into stereotyping, you're getting Mama all wrong! She and I have talked a lot recently about the so-called "religious right." We've discussed how some people today seem to be trying to make Jesus look pro-war, pro-rich, trying to use Jesus to teach hatred of those who are different from us. (Race, nationality, sexual orientation, and religion were among the differences we discussed.) She concluded that conversation emphatically with the proclamation, *"That's not the Jesus I know!"* Among the Biblical allusions she made were Jesus teaching that it was the *peacemakers* who were called the children of God, that Jesus constantly talked about helping the poor (and how hard it was for the rich to get into Heaven), and that Jesus taught us to love *all* people, even our enemies. It's clear to me there's wisdom in that approach!

Race is another area in which Mom has been for many years a positive influence on me. See, I love the small towns of the South, like Greenwood. I love the smallness, the friendliness, the neighborliness, the food, the family focus, the values, the whole culture. Well, *almost* the whole culture. I never liked gossip much, but it does seem to be part of the package, doesn't it? But my point is racism. I grew up with a lot of it! I heard the n-word a lot in Greenwood. But I never heard it from my Mother! Indeed, I remember one occasion when I came home from school upset about what kids were saying about the Rev. Dr. Martin Luther King, Jr.—"Communist," "trouble-making nigger," etc. I talked to Mama about it, and two things stand out in my memory. First, she said "Davie, we have to listen to that man, you know—he's a Baptist preacher." It meant a lot to me then, and somehow means even more to me now, that even as King led the civil rights movement that was shaking the very foundation of the social order of the South, including Greenwood, Mom was able to see the good. The other thing that stands out in my memory is how the conversation ended: "You'd better not ever let me hear of *you* calling him names like that!" Wisdom. Rising above bigotry, in this case—and helping me to do so.

When I started to college at Eastern New Mexico University in the fall of 1958, and for the first time in my life was exposed to diversity—including Native Americans, African Americans, and Hispanic Americans—I was not totally unprepared, thanks in large part to Mom. And by the way, speaking of college: I've always been convinced that one of the reasons Mom has always been so supportive of my educational endeavors, through graduate school to the Ph.D. and becoming a history professor, is that she was vicariously experiencing it for herself.

Mother impresses me, among other ways, with her continuing intellectual curiosity. How many 93-year olds do you know who will ask questions like, "What is all this dot com stuff, anyway?" Or "What do you think about gay marriage?" Or who will suggest that some of the people who want to violate the principle of separation of church and state by posting the Ten Commandments everywhere don't really pay much attention to what some of the Ten Commandments *say*. She made it clear in this latter conversation that she was talking about "Thou shalt not kill," and the fact that some folks will complain about restrictions on where the Commandments can be posted while at the same time supporting such things as war and capital punishment.

That's my Sebastian County Mother. Or at least that's *part* of my Sebastian County Mother. She is a rich, complex character. Does she have her limits? Of course. Don't we all? Just one example: I remember, back in the 80s, trying to talk to her about feminine images of God, something I was all excited about at the time. She didn't want to hear it, *wouldn't* hear it. So I dropped it. Hey, my Mama didn't raise no dummies!

So, if you're ever in Booneville, Arkansas (I know, I know, that's way over in Logan County!), go by the Oak Manor Nursing and Rehabilitation Center and have a visit with Mama. Her name is Gladys Marie Davis Joyce. She loves company. You'll enjoy it too. And you might even gain some wisdom.

CHAPTER 2

Race, The Rebel Flag, And My Home Town: A Rant

Some years ago, I had a surgical procedure that temporarily affected my vocal chords so that all I could do for some time was whisper. My wife tells me that as I came out from under the anesthetic, I whispered "I hate the fucking Confederate flag!" She said, "Okay, sweetheart, you rest now." I have no idea why that was on my mind at the moment. But I *do* hate that flag!

If you stick with me and read this, you'll get a lot more of my opinions, but let me start with a couple of *facts* (I am a *historian*, after all). In the American Civil War, 1861-1865, if the people who marched into battle carrying that flag had been successful, my country, the United States of America, as it then existed, would have been severed/destroyed. And if the people who marched into battle carrying that flag had been successful, the evil of human slavery would have been protected/expanded/ perpetuated. I am *not* necessarily saying that's what the people carrying that flag had in mind, okay? I was never much into psychohistory even when it was a fad. We have enough trouble trying to figure out people's motives for anything *now*, and I would argue we simply cannot do it with historical figures. But I do argue that those two statements about destroying the US and perpetuating slavery are indisputably factual.

When my wife and I lived in Hungary for two years, from 1994 to 1996, twice there were incidents in the "big forest" of Debrecen near the university where I taught in which skinhead racist thugs beat up people who were not white enough to suit them. According to witnesses, both times, the perpetrators were wearing black leather jackets with, you guessed it, the "Confederate" flag emblazoned upon them. They knew what that flag symbolized, didn't they? Even according to Alexander H. Stephens, the Vice President of the so-called Confederate States of America, race was at the heart of their endeavor. Referring to the Confederate government, he said: "...its foundations are laid, its corner-stone rests, upon the great truth that the negro is not equal to the white man, that slavery—subordination to the superior race—is his natural and normal condition."

You know, you can't really remove a symbol, like a flag, from its historical context. Try putting a German Nazi swastika bumper sticker on your pickup and when somebody calls you on it, saying "Oh, no, it doesn't mean all *that*, it's just German pride." Yea, right.

You see, I had the incredible experience of being *asked* to write a piece for the county historical society newsletter of my home town of Greenwood, Arkansas, then having it *rejected* because I dealt honestly with the issue of race. Maybe I should not have been surprised? Greenwood, after all, made it to James Loewen's book, *Sundown Towns*, a painful, insightful book about towns with a history of ugly racism, specifically with a history of keeping African Americans out of town after sunset. I remember a class reunion at which a much-revered coach told a joke about the first African American astronaut. The punch line? "The jig's up!" And recently, while there dealing with the death of my mother, in the Bulldog Diner (the high school team mascot is Bulldogs, and on the wall are pictures of my Mother as the first Homecoming Queen in 1929 and of my brother and me as part of basketball teams back in the day), I saw a poster prominently displayed over by the cash register, a poster of Barack Obama computer-enhanced to look like a Muslim terrorist—specifically to look as much like Osama bin Laden as possible. At the top were the words, "So you say you want change, America?" and at the bottom, "Get ready!" I told the staff how offensive, inappropriate, and ignorant I found the poster, but I fear my response represents a tiny minority of those who go in there. The cousin (yes, cousin) who invited me to write the piece for the newsletter even acknowledged at the end of the ugly incident that maybe things hadn't changed as much in Greenwood as elsewhere. Here, in its entirety, is the essay I submitted:

Reflections on Growing Up in
Greenwood, Sebastian County, Arkansas

I am very proud to be from Greenwood! At some points in my life, when I'd say that to some people, they would clearly wonder "Why?" I suspect most readers of this piece will understand.

I love the small towns of the South, like Greenwood. I love the smallness, the friendliness, the neighborliness, the food, the family focus, the values, the whole culture.

I never liked the gossip much that seems to go along with all that, but it does seem to be part of the package, doesn't it? I remember being in a conversation once at Christmastime in Greenwood with Charles Angeletti and C. O. Bell, Jr., not long after each of us had gone through a divorce. C. O. started laughing, with no apparent relationship to anything said. We asked him what was so funny. He said, "I was just thinking, if lightning struck this place right now and killed the three of us, Greenwood wouldn't have anything to gossip about for years."

I retired from full-time teaching last year (as a history professor, mostly at the University of Tulsa and East Central University, in Ada, Oklahoma). My wife, Carole, and I are now living on Lake Spavinaw northeast of Tulsa. Spavinaw's a very small town, probably about 500. There's one café, the Greenhorn. Other than being a beautiful spot—hills, trees, creeks, the lake (very much like Arkansas!)—one of the things I enjoy is the small town flavor. I like hanging out at the Greenhorn Café early in the morning after taking a walk down by the lake, to drink coffee and gossip (oops!) with the locals. I've even met an old fellow there, Al Boyer, with ties to Greenwood! (His wife was Bernice Wright; she's buried at Liberty Cemetery, right where my Daddy—Albert Arthur "Bud" Joyce—and sister —Rose Marilyn Joyce Geren—are buried; and Al plans to be as well. I enjoy those kinds of connections.)

But I've run into one thing here in Spavinaw that reminds me of the other thing I don't like, far more serious than gossip, about the South and its small towns—including, unfortunately, Greenwood. I'm talking about bigotry. I'm talking about comments like "I don't watch no TV anymore; there ain't nothin' on there but niggers and queers," which I overheard in an adjoining booth at the Greenhorn. And the suggestion that the American soldier accused during the recent war against Iraq of attacking his own men "looks like either a sand nigger or a real nigger." I was actually *in* the four-way conversation when that offensive line was uttered. I still struggle with the best way to respond. Do you speak up, probably causing a scene and not changing anybody's mind? Or do you bite your tongue and remain silent, thus perhaps giving the impression that kind of language is no problem to you?

In Greenwood, I remember hearing the *n*-word a lot. But I never heard it from my mother! That's just one of the ways Gladys Marie Davis Joyce (Greenwood's first Homecoming Queen!) was a positive influence on me. I remember going home from school one day upset about what kids were saying about the Rev. Dr. Martin Luther King, Jr.—"Communist," "trouble-making nigger," etc. I talked to Mama about it; she said, "Davie, we have to listen to that man, you know—he's a Baptist preacher." I have always been amazed that even as he led the civil rights movement that was shaking the very foundation of the social order of the South, including Greenwood, Mama was able to see the good. (Of course, she also once told a guy at the Baptist church who had said that if there were going to be "niggers" in heaven, he didn't want to go there, that she thought he didn't need to worry about it because she was pretty sure with that attitude, he wouldn't make it!)

One of the many things I look back on positively about Greenwood is my educational experience. Teachers like Mrs. Craig, Mrs. Been, Mrs. Bedrosian—in my view, it would have been hard to have better anywhere! Getting older, when old things are sometimes fresher in our memories than recent things, I have vivid images of my experiences in their classrooms. They prepared me well, as I look back on it, for college, graduate school, and a life in teaching.

I have strong memories of Mr. King's 10th-grade United States history class, as well. But some of the reasons there may be a bit different. I remember that Mr. King had a leather strap with holes in it for punishment purposes. I remember that he was about to give Billy Craig five lashes with it for some offense. I remember that several of us spoke up in complaint. I remember that he put us on the spot, saying basically, "Okay, if five of you boys feel strongly enough about this that you want to take a lick each for Billy, line up." We did! (In my memory, it was Ralph Vines, Tommy Basham, C. O. Bell, Wayne Lowe, and me. But I also know that those vivid memories we *think* we have of old times are sometimes of doubtful veracity! So if this is wrong, I'm sorry.) There's a lesson there, perhaps, but I'm not sure what it is —or what it has to do with US history! Something about a small town value of standing up for your friends, maybe?

As I became increasingly interested in reading, especially history, Daddy couldn't really relate, couldn't, I think, quite understand why I didn't take up the interest in cattle he had and that my older brother, Danny Bruce Joyce, did take up. (I learned important values from him too, though; somehow the first one that comes to mind is honesty.) But Mom encouraged me. And so did teachers. In some ways, I think, so did Greenwood itself. Somehow I developed this belief, which at the end of thirty-something years of teaching/reading/writing history I still hold, that it's fundamentally important in knowing who you *are* to know where you came from—that past, present, and future are not separate things, but part of a continuum, blending into each other, informing each other. (History has even helped me understand bigotry. But not to accept it.) My past was in Greenwood, Arkansas. My experience there helped make me what I am. A person could do a lot worse!

I struggle when I go to Greenwood today. Ever since "The Tornado"—which, among other things, wiped out the court house, for many Greenwood's most distinctive landmark—it hasn't looked or felt much like the home town I remember. But overall, I'm still really proud to say "I'm from Greenwood,

Arkansas, in Sebastian County, near Ft. Smith. I was born in the area that's now Ft. Chaffee . . . ."

That's it. And it was rejected. And it was made clear that it was rejected specifically because of the portions that dealt with race. As I said, the cousin informed me that "attitudes probably haven't changed as much in Greenwood as they have in the rest of the country." The Editorial Review Board, he said, "flinched" when they got to the two paragraphs on bigotry. (*Not*, apparently, because it was painful to be reminded of the bigotry that *used* to exist, please notice, but because of the bigotry that *still* existed!) Needless to say, I flinched when I read the rejection! As a life-long scholar, I've published numerous books, book reviews, articles, etc., and certainly I've had my share of rejections. But this one felt unique! He suggested I could either replace the two offending paragraphs with some "happy thoughts" of my choosing, or they could simply leave out the two paragraphs and print the rest. I said, basically: I haven't spent my career studying/reading/writing/teaching a white-washed version of history, and I certainly won't engage in it in my county historical society newsletter. At my insistence, the essay was returned.

Has Greenwood changed? Well, I'm sorry to say, I still don't think so. I mentioned the anti-Obama poster in a restaurant in Greenwood in 2008. I should also mention an event at the Greenwood rodeo in 2012. Apparently, an effigy of President Obama was knocked around by a bull and then kicked by a clown. While some people were reportedly unhappy about the disrespect for the President, it must be noted that the announcer himself got in on the "fun," shouting out "Who wants to rip Obama's head off?" (Though in all fairness, it should be noted that there is an occasional reason for hope. I have learned that there are several black cemeteries in the area that are in bad shape, but members of the Norwood family, one of Greenwood's old black families, along with the local Boy Scout troop and the South Sebastian County Historical Society, are at work restoring them.)

Also, James Loewen's *Sundown Towns*, while not dealing with Greenwood specifically as one of the towns with a history of keeping blacks out of town after sunset, is mentioned—and in an ugly way. Loewen quotes an African American college student saying to him and a group of students in 2002 at the University of the Ozarks in Clarksville, "Never walk in Greenwood or you will die." To be careful here, Loewen introduces that story by noting that, "Even after the turn of the millennium, there were . . . still towns that African Americans believed were not safe simply to pass through." Note the qualifier "believed." Is it true? Loewen notes that the 2000 census listed 17 African Americans in Greenwood, including two households, "so perhaps his [the student's] information was out of date." Perhaps. I have a cousin who's a retired school teacher in Greenwood. I asked her about this, specifically blacks in the Greenwood schools. She replied that some of the students were "products of interracial marriages." She told a beautiful story about a black girl in high school who tried out for and got the part of the fairy godmother in a production of "Cinderella." And she said "I have never seen any problems with any of the students who are in school here and have been in school here because they are black." But she also told me about a black boy who was taunted by being called "nigger" numerous times.

But in many ways perhaps Greenwood is not so different from the rest of the South—or the rest of the country. Bob Herbert, writing in the *New York Times* in 2007 (March 1) insisted accurately:

> There's a great deal that Americans don't fully understand about slavery. It's such an uncomfortable subject that the temptation is to relegate it to the distant past and move on. But the long tentacles of that evil institution are still with us. Slavery was the foundation of the thriving consumer society that we have today and the wellspring of the racism that still poisons so many white attitudes and black lives.

Interestingly, the occasion for Herbert's piece was the discovery by the Rev. Al Sharpton that his family had once been owned by the family of archsegregationist Senator Strom Thurmond—*and* that they were cousins! Herbert went further:

> Instead of reaping rewards for [their] seminal role in the creation of a rich and powerful nation, blacks have been relentlessly vilified by a profoundly racist society and frozen out

of most of the nation's bounty. Consigned to the bottom of the caste heap after emancipation, and denied some of the most basic human rights, blacks became the convenient depository of whatever blame and negative stereotypes whites chose to cast their way.

The abject state ruthlessly imposed upon blacks for so long became, perversely, proof of their inferiority. Blacks gave whites of all classes someone to look down upon. Slavery, like the past, as Faulkner reminded us, is not dead. It's not even past. It's not something that you can wish away.

Back, specifically, to the "Rebel" flag, and the so-called Confederate States of America. Why, you might wonder, do I always refer to "so-called Confederacy" or place it in quotes? Because I agree with Abraham Lincoln: Those who *attempted* to secede from the US and set up a new government did not have the right to do so, never really succeeded in doing so. (I used to like to say to students that the Southern states never really succeeded in seceding—but I'm not sure they got it.) The CSA was never a legitimate government. Those who supported it were committing treason and rebellion—and all in the name of slavery.

I've paid a lot of attention to popular music over the years. I even taught a course several times on Rock and Roll in American History, in which I tried to place the music in context with what was going on politically/socially/culturally. (It also provided an excuse to listen to a lot of good tunes in class!) And while I have found myself liking a lot of music that came out of the South, I was always terribly uncomfortable with the whole Southern Rock sub-culture that was too frequently symbolized by the Confederate flag. Suffice it to say that in the confrontation between Neil Young and Lynrd Skynrd, I side with Neil Young. He wrote, in "Southern Man:"

> Southern man better keep your head
> Don't forget what your good book said
>
> Southern change gonna come at last
> Now your crosses are burning fast
> Southern man
>
> I saw cotton and I saw black
> Tall white mansions and little shacks.
> Southern man when will you pay them back?

> I heard screamin and bullwhips cracking
> How long? How long?

Lynrd Skynrd, one of the best known of the "Southern rock bands," answered back in "Sweet Home Alabama:"

> Well I heard mister Young sing about her
> Well, I heard ole Neil put her down
> Well, I hope Neil Young will remember
>   Southern man don't need him around anyhow

It's clear to me the Southerner *still* needs critiquing by outsiders, after all these years. And insiders like myself as well!

A couple more songs, less known, have something to say here as well. Jason Ringenberg, of the band Jason and the (Nashville) Scorchers, was riding on a train in central Germany when he saw the "omnipresent rebel flag" on a barn. He wrote a song about it, "Rebel Flag in Germany," in which he sang:

> Well I reckon I can tell you that Robert E. Lee
> Would not have wished to see his flag in central Germany
> I wish I'd never seen that flag in central Germany
> Hell I don't even want to see that flag in Tennessee

Sarah Lee Guthrie, granddaughter of the great Woody Guthrie and daughter of Arlo, and her husband Johnny Irion, make a contribution as well, with their song "Gervais," in which they sang "Was a battleflag, now we can put it away." Yes, that's it, put it away—a *museum*, now that's a place I wouldn't mind seeing the "Confederate" flag.

While I was working on this chapter, my good friend Al Turner showed once again that he knows me quite well by sending me a song by Mike West called "Dixie"—and no, it's not *that* "Dixie." Here are some of the words:

> I don't go in that bar since they eighty-sixed me
> for throwin' a drink that the waitress fixed me
> at a customer who asked for "Dixie"
> I don't suffer fools and I don't play "Dixie"
>
> See that statue, that's general e. lee
> they should knock him on his ass if you ask me
> I ain't no gray coat as you can see
> I don't suffer fools and I don't play "Dixie"
>
> You show your true colors, well I'll show mine
> but I'll warn you now boo

> my colors they're more red than white and blue
> if you don't like it, go ahead and hit me
> but I don't suffer fools and I don't play "Dixie"

Not designed to win friends and influence people, I suppose, but as Al guessed, it is a "Dixie" I could play comfortably if I were a musician.

Also while I was working on this chapter, a piece came out in the *Tulsa World* (May 1, 2011) by columnist Richard Cohen of the Washington Post Syndicate which supports my views on this subject. "It's the Lee myth that's lost," read the headline. Cohen began by noting that "the Lee legend—swaddled in myth, kitsch and racism—has endured even past the civil rights era when it became both urgent and right to finally tell the 'Lost Cause' to get lost. Now it should be Lee's turn. He was loyal to slavery and disloyal to his country...." Noting that Lee owned slaves himself and "fought tenaciously in the courts to keep them," Cohen insisted more broadly—and accurately—that Lee also "commanded a vast army that, had it won, would have secured the independence of a nation dedicated to the proposition that white people could own black people and sell them off, husband from wife, child from parent, as the owner saw fit. Such a man cannot be admired." Cohen noted that when he moved to the Washington, DC, area, he "used to marvel" at the homages to Lee, especially in his home state of Virginia, and wonder "What was being honored? Slavery? Treason?" Cohen acknowledges a recent book by Elizabeth Brown Pryor entitled *Reading the Man: A Portrait of Robert E. Lee Through His Private Letters*. Pryor gives us, says Cohen, "a Lee who is at odds with the one of gauzy myth." After the Civil War, he says, "the South embraced a mythology of victimhood. An important feature was the assertion that the war had been not about slavery at all but about state's rights. The secessionists themselves were not so shy. In their various declarations, they announced they were leaving the Union to preserve slavery. Lee not only accepted the Lost Cause myth, he propagated it and came to embody it." In that "exotic place called the antebellum South," concludes Cohen, "there were plenty of people who recognized the evil of slavery or, if nothing else, the folly of secession. Lee was not one of them. He deserves no honor . . . he fought on the wrong side for the wrong cause.

It's time for Virginia and the South to honor the ones who were right."

There's a couple in Greenwood that I love so much. But we know we're poles apart ideologically, specifically in politics and religion. So, as is so often the case, we basically just don't talk about it. But once the South did come up. I can't remember the details of the specific story I was responding to, but I do remember saying "Thank God the South *did* lose the Civil War." That led to both of them jumping on me and telling me it had *nothing* to do with slavery. I *wanted* to say it had *everything* to do with slavery, and that it's hard to find a professional historian anymore who doesn't realize that. I wanted to talk about the 3/5 Compromise in the Constitution itself, giving Southern slaveholders an unfair advantage all the way up to the Civil War in the federal government. I wanted to tell about the Missouri Compromise, the Compromise of 1850, the Kansas-Nebraska act, etc.—all of which show the centrality of slavery, and specifically its expansion, to the coming of the Civil War. I wanted to show how slavery was at the *heart* of all the other differences between North and South, like economics, religion, states' rights (if *that* was really the South's concern, then why didn't Southern political leaders support the right of *Northern* states to find ways to off-set the to-them obnoxious Fugitive Slave Law that required them to help return escaped slaves? Wonder if that had anything to do with states' rights harming *slavery* in that case?!). But I didn't tell them any of that. Should I have? I was shocked, hurt. Yes, hurt. Kind of like being invited to write an essay and then having it rejected because of its honesty. I mean, they were not willing/able to respect me, either as friend or as professional historian who has spent an entire career studying/ reading/teaching/writing this stuff, to listen to me. ("My mind's made up; don't confuse me with the facts.") I *think* my on-the-spot motive in not pushing it further was that I decided the human connection was more important; I didn't want to hurt my relationship with them. I still don't know if that was the right thing to do.

(As I was writing this essay, trying to bring it to a close, my state representative came to the door, campaigning. He's a conservative Republican. In case it's not obvious by now, I'm not. My main problem with the Democratic party, especially here in Oklahoma, is that they are not far enough *left* on the political spectrum to suit me.. But we had a good conversation. I think he's a nice guy. It's pretty clear he thinks I am as well. He even bought some of my books a couple of years ago, though clearly he doesn't *agree* with me on much of anything, including American history and Oklahoma history. I told him I might vote for him. I think he's a person of integrity. I also think—the real point here—that it's important that we be willing/able to reach out across the barriers of politics, religion, whatever, that we so often allow to divide us, and treat each other with sincere respect, and try to learn from each other. Indeed, I'm afraid that's not happening often enough these days.)

So I guess I've long had a somewhat problematic relationship with the South. As I noted in the reprinted essay above, there's so much about it that I love, including family, food, friendliness. But as I wrote a few years ago to a good friend: "But it's deeply flawed (aren't all sections? aren't all PEOPLE?)." Sometimes I've said that I love the South—well, except for that whole slavery/ racism/treason thing. But then it occurs to me that's a bit like saying I'm really quite healthy—well, except for the fact that I'm dying of cancer.

I do know this: My *language* may have been inappropriate that day after the surgery. (Certainly my Mother, whom you know a bit from the first chapter, would never have approved its use! And if any reader is bothered by it, never fear, you will not read it again in these pages.) But my *sentiments* were stated accurately—and I still do hate the "Confederate" flag.

⊛

Afterword to a Rant

I shared an early draft of this essay with one of my Hungarian friends, Tibor Glant, and he suggested I use this quote from Adolph Hitler: "Since the Civil War, in which the Southern States were conquered against all historical logic and sound sense, the Americans have been in a condition of political and popular decay. In that war, it was not the Southern States, but the American people themselves who were conquered. [. . .]

The beginnings of a great new social order based on the principle of slavery and inequality were destroyed in that war, and with them also the embryo of a future truly great America that would not have been ruled by a corrupt caste of tradesmen, but by a real Herren-class that would have swept away all the falsities of liberty and equality." There, how's that for praise for the so-called Confederacy?!

An e-mail exchange with another friend, Tom Richardson, also seems appropriate to share here. Tom is not a historian, but, admirably, has been trying to learn some history in recent years. On the Civil War era, I suggested he read James McPherson's Pulitzer Prize-winning work, *Battle Cry of Freedom*. "I am not interested in all the battle stuff," he said, "having read a lot on that point. I am really interested in what caused the division. Was it all slavery? [. . .] Was it the small land owners in New England vs the large plantation owners which used slaves? Was it cultural and religious? Jefferson professed that he was opposed to slavery, perhaps fostered children with them, but then kept his slaves. I assume so that he could keep his large estate. These are some of the issues I would like to explore further."

I responded: "A few quick thoughts from yours truly: I agree about the battles; for me, that's the LEAST interesting part of the Civil War, and, as I recall, McPherson is not TOO heavy on that. Was it 'all' slavery? No. But slavery was essential to all the other differences, and, in the end, the one North and South could not resolve peacefully. [. . .] Yes, it was economic. Free small farmers versus big land-holding slave-working plantation owners. But notice the crucial difference there: free labor versus slave labor. Yes, it was cultural. And in many ways those cultural differences reflected geography, both physical and human. (Where did the people COME from to North and South, and what cultural baggage did they bring with them?) But the central cultural difference? Free vs slave. Northerners became increasingly anti-slavery; Southerners, even those who didn't own slaves (the vast majority) became increasingly attached to slavery. (Some of the worst racism came from non-slave owning Southerners . . . 'hey, at least I ain't no slave'—while it's easy to show that they were EXPLOITED themselves by the dominance of slavery.) Was it religious? Yes. But Northern ministers increasingly preached the freedom of the gospel, and supported the anti-slavery movement (including some Unitarians, I'm proud to say), while Southern ministers increasingly supported slavery, and tried to use the Bible to do so. Jefferson's a tough nut to crack. Was he sincere in his Declaration of Independence rhetoric about freedom/liberty/equality? I think so. (Though notice how hard–impossible?–it is to determine the sincerity/ motivation of historical figures.) Did he 'think' women and Blacks when he wrote it? I think not. Was he imperfect? Aren't all humans? Did he father children with one of his slaves? Almost certainly. How interesting does THAT make his dilemma? Personalizing it in an incredibly powerful way. You didn't mention 'Constitutional' issues, but I'm going to briefly. Powerful Southern slaveowners got an unfair advantage at the Constitutional Convention and in the Constitution itself. The 3/5 Compromise? Gimme a break! It meant that they, disregarding the unfair advantage that gave them all the way down to the Civil War (being REWARDED for OWNING fellow human beings), they cried about how they were treated by the federal government, and increasingly called for 'states' rights' (read: leave us alone and let us keep our slaves). And also let us EXPAND slavery. Because it's clear to me that THAT is the political form the issue took which led to the Civil War . . . Southern slaveholders demanding the right to EXPAND their 'peculiar institution' into the West, in part because their exploitative system (exploiting land AND humans) had worn out the land. WAS it states' rights in any meaningful way other than protecting slavery? I think not. Look at how the so-called 'Confederacy' treated states' rights. (By the way, it was their VP, Alexander H. Stephens, who said that race was the foundation for the CSA.) And earlier, if Southern political leaders were so enamored of states' rights, why didn't they support the efforts of NORTHERN states to off-set the Fugitive Slave Law of 1850? Because it got in the way of their efforts to get their escaped slaves back! So the issue? Not states' rights at all, but slavery.

Well, I said brief. I lied. I feel strongly about all this, which is probably obvious. So you've got some history and some of my stuff. But my stuff is soundly based, I believe, on history. Besides, Howard Zinn taught me that 'objectivity' is a myth, neither possible nor desirable. It's inevitable that the way we see history is influenced by our 'climate of opinion,' our race/age/gender/ ideology/time/place/etc. In conclusion, though, Tom, I would say this: The BASICS of the viewpoint I've outlined here are broadly accepted in the historical profession, and have been for a long time, to the point that it's hard to find a respectable professional historian who would NOT agree on the centrality of slavery. It's like, folks at the TIME of the Civil War had no doubt it was about slavery, but historians went through all these different cycles of interpretation before finally coming back to the realization that, oh, you know what . . . it was all about slavery!"

Chapter 3

Willie Morris' North Toward Home
A Personal Response

As I talked with friends about the possibility of a more
"personal/historical" book such as this one, two of them,
Charles Angeletti and Mike Nobles, independently came up with
the idea of having me read *North Toward Home*, by Willie Morris.
(Charles is a long-time history professor at Metropolitan State
College of Denver, Colorado, Mike a retired labor organizer in
Tulsa, Oklahoma, and lover of dogs and books, co-founder with
his wife Kathy of A Gathering of Writers.) Clearly, they both felt
Morris' exploration of his ambivalent relationship with his
hometown of Yazoo City, Mississippi, might help me explore my
relationship with my hometown of Greenwood, Arkansas. After
you read this chapter, you can decide for yourself if they were
right.

Morris divides his story into three parts geographically—
Mississippi, Texas, and New York. For me, it would be Arkansas,
New Mexico, and Oklahoma. Essentially, that means he was
from Mississippi, me from Arkansas, he went to school in Texas,
me in New Mexico, and he settled in to live in New York, me in
Oklahoma.

I only had to make it to page ten in my reading of *North
Toward Home* to see that Charles and Mike might be onto
something. Morris spoke of his uncle by marriage, Henry S.
Foote, his "true family hero." Clearly, one of the things Morris
liked about Foote was that he was "one of those authentic
nineteenth-century Southern-Americans, a fighter for the Union,

an uncompromising enemy of the Southern extremists," and specifically that he "had the unequivocal good judgment to hold Jefferson Davis in low esteem."

Sometimes Morris' experience rings a bell for me, but in an opposite way, so to speak. He writes of an apparently significant African American population in Yazoo City, and the fact that his Mother reprimanded him severely on one occasion for playing with children there. "Don't ever play back here again," he quotes her saying as she yanked him home. "But why?" he asked. "Just you hear me. Just you don't" was her only reply. Greenwood had no significant Black population, just a couple named Jim and Fanny as I recall who lived in the woods north of town and who had no children for us to be tempted to play with—or who wanted to go to school with us—thus they seemed somehow okay. But you know how different my Mother was from Morris' Mother on the Black issue from stories I've already told.

Religion was obviously important in Morris' early life, a particular brand of white Southern Protestantism that resonates with my experience to a certain extent. "There was a war on for my salvation," he writes, and goes on to speak of revivals, Vacation Bible Schools, etc., all of which were part of my experience as well. He writes that when he hears "church bells on some lonely, cold Sunday morning on Manhattan Island," he feels "a touch of guilt, and the remorseless pull of my precocious piety." With those lines, Morris reminded me of the Susan Werner song, "Sunday Mornings," in which she sings:

> sunday morning
> there is someplace that i'm supposed to be
> keeps returning
> the feeling keeps coming over me
> just like music
> or like sunlight on a distant memory
> sunday morning
> sunday morning
>
> and i went back the other day
> closed my eyes and tried to pray
> but a voice spoke loud and clear
> "you ask too many questions, dear"
> and i said, "you ask too few"
> that's why i still don't know quite what to do
> on sunday mornings.

Fortunately, I don't have that problem. While my faith evolved in a different direction from that of my Mom and Dad, I do have one, Unitarian Universalism, and you'll read more about it in Chapter 8. The religious spectrum in Greenwood, as I remember it, was pretty narrow, consisting of Methodist, Baptist, Presbyterian, Church of Christ, and Assembly of God. Mom was a Baptist, Dad a Methodist. Until age 12, my brother and sister and I had a choice, not whether to go to church, of course, but whether to go to the Methodist with Dad or the Baptist with Mom. And *at* age 12, we had a choice, not whether to join a church, of course, but which of those two to join. My brother and I chose Methodist, my sister Baptist. I should add that I still have a deep and abiding respect for my Mother's Southern Baptist faith, having seen how it helped carry her through the hardest of times right up until her death.

Morris makes reference to reading books not really being an acceptable form of "intellection" in his case. As for me, I do believe my Dad had trouble figuring out why I wanted to read books (and practice my cornet) instead of working with the cows, his lifelong job and passion, but my Mother encouraged my reading, as she later encouraged my education.

Morris also remembers "spending long hours in the cemetery." I remember that as well, but the cemetery thing never really caught with me—I plan to be cremated. I do have vivid memories of "Decoration Day," when everyone from Greenwood would come back and go to the cemetery and place flowers on the graves of their loved ones. I even remember seeing Gene Autry there once! I was a fan, of course, of his movies, so I got all excited. My Grandmother, Beulah Davis, told me he was a distant cousin! Turns out he was putting flowers on the grave of someone named Autry Davis, suggesting a connection between the two families.

I mentioned being a fan of Gene Autry movies; more broadly, I grew up loving westerns. Thus, no surprise that I also loved a song called "Saturday Matinee" by Larry Ballard from 1974. He has verses that eulogize Lash LaRue, the Cisco Kid, and Hopalong Cassidy, in addition to Gene Autry, and sings in the chorus:

> So take me back just for a day
> Back to that same old front row seat at the Saturday matinee
> Popcorn and Baby Ruths and all that junk I'd eat
> No matter how many cokes I drank I never left my seat

Though he goes a bit further than I would when he ends:

> So take me back and Lord when I die
> Just give me that same old front row seat
> At that big matinee in the sky

I don't remember my family being very highly political. But to the extent they were, their politics were considerably different from Morris' folks. He remembers his Dad being intensely anti-Franklin D. Roosevelt. I remember, on the other hand, my Mom and Dad thinking you should never consider voting any way other than Democratic because FDR saved the country, helped lead us to victory in World War II, etc. Indeed, I think my earliest memory of "historical events," defined as things which go beyond your own home, friends, etc., was the death of FDR. I would have been only four years old, so concepts like "death" and "President" wouldn't have meant much to me, but I seem to remember everybody being sad. Not too long later, I remember the end of the war. I had turned five by then, but even so, mostly I remember personalizing the event—"Alright, Uncle Harvey and Uncle D. W. are coming home!" They were my Dad's two brothers, the first serving in the Navy, the second in the Army. Harvey went on to a career in the Navy; D. W., on the other hand, was deeply traumatized by his experience, especially the parts where he wound up on "clean-up squads" sent into POW camps, concentration camps, etc.

Morris makes reference to "the horrific gossip of a small town." I remember it vividly—it was, and still is, one of my least favorite things about small-town Southern life. He remembers one Baptist preacher who was especially noted for his tirades against sex. Morris says he was so affected by the message that "I was in some doubt as to whether I should ever touch myself, much less anybody else." It's my belief that most males of Southern Protestant upbringing in those days, if they were being honest, would admit to having some adjustments to go through before reaching a healthy, happy sex life. And alcohol? Mississippi, notes Morris, was a dry state; so was Arkansas. One of the absolute worst sins, right up there with sex before marriage and dancing, was drinking. I didn't try it until college, and feel that I had more problems with it because of my "prohibitionist" upbringing than I would have with a healthy exposure to it.

Morris remembers hunting squirrels, etc., but not deer; "my father was against it," he notes. I'm not sure my Father was against it, but I don't remember it being a part of my life like it was for so many of the boys I grew up with. And as for myself? At about age 10, I'd say, I did talk Mom and Dad into letting me have a BB gun. And the first time I tried to shoot a bird, I succeeded. Then I started crying! I'm not entirely sure why, but as I look back on it, I think it was at that moment that I realized hunting was not for me! I also think all this had something to do with my tendency toward vegetarianism—though seeing cattle slaughtered at the slaughter house in Fort Smith could have been a factor as well!

Deer hunting reminds me of another book Charles Angeletti insisted I read, Joe Bageant's *Deer Hunting with Jesus: Dispatches from America's Class War*. And while it was an interesting read, and helped me understand why some working class whites hate liberalism (and maybe even how a left-wing guy could love guns), it did not get the juices flowing as Morris did. At times, it reminded me of Thomas Frank's *What's the Matter with Kansas?* Certainly it helps the reader understand that the white working class has been ravaged by the very party, Republican, that claims to take their side. But it goes further, and is very different in tone, hilarious at times, offensive at times, but something of a call to arms for fellow progressives with little real understanding of "the great beery, NASCAR-loving, church-going, gun-owning America that has never set foot in a Starbucks." Bageant writes of a minister in his hometown of Winchester, Virginia, to which he chose to move back, "He would say that my soul is troubling me and that I need to be washed in the blood and redeemed by the grace of him who bled for our sins. I'd say that I am troubled by the distinct impression of approaching trihorned fascism—part Christian, part military, part corporate." I'd say I'm more with Bageant on that one. I am, however, very uncomfortable when he seems to be making fun, as in his suggestion of the folks in his favorite café in Winchester that "Even if they took the trouble to read George Orwell's *Animal Farm*, none of them would see it as anything other than a story about animals." I've long found it very troubling and arrogant to assume of those with whom we differ that if they just understood, they'd agree.

Back to Willie Morris. "Like Mark Twain and his comrades growing up a century before in another village on the other side of the Mississippi," he writes, "my friends and I had but one sustaining ambition in the 1940s. Theirs in Hannibal was to be steamboatmen, ours in Yazoo was to be major-league baseball players." I can identify with that! I remember hearing the St. Louis Cardinals on the radio everywhere I went as I grew up; I even remember a friend hollowing out the pages of a book and inserting an early version of a transistor radio so we could listen to the World Series in 10th grade English class! Baseball caught on for me personally so much that I took advantage of the opportunity to coach a baseball team when I was teaching at a university in Hungary in the 1990s, and my wife Carole and I have seen at least one game in all thirty Major League cities!

As a teenager, Morris had brief experience as a writer and a disc jockey. So did I. The writing proved to be very important, as I look back on it. Mrs. Bedrosian, my 10th grade English teacher, had us write a short story. Influenced by science fiction that I had discovered on band trips, I wrote one about a robot that started thinking for itself. Mrs. Bedrosian encouraged me to revise it a bit and submit it for a competition held by the Beta Club, our version of an honor society. I did so, and received "Honorable Mention"—and publication! I had never dreamed that I might be capable of writing something someone else might want to read. Later, thanks in part to that experience, starting to publish as a part of my career somehow felt natural. Morris' experience as a disc jockey was clearly more extensive than mine, and earlier in his life, as it took place in Yazoo City, while mine did not occur until I had left Greenwood to go to college in New Mexico and was limited to filling in for a friend for short periods of time. I wasn't even a paid employee. But I do remember feeling pretty cool saying "Hi, this is DJ your DJ . . . ."

Approaching high school graduation, says Morris, he was advised by his Father to "get the hell out of Mississippi." I definitely do not remember my Father telling me to get out of Arkansas. Indeed, like Morris with Mississippi, "I saw no reason to leave." Asthma, however, provided that reason for me. He remembers vividly being "sick with leaving for the first time the place where I grew up," and catching a bus in Vicksburg for Austin, Texas, to attend the university there. I remember leaving Greenwood vividly also. The doctors felt I needed a higher and dryer climate for my breathing problems, so Mom and Dad and I worked out for me to hitch a ride with a cousin, and his wife, who was in the Air Force and stationed at Clovis Air Force Base in New Mexico, where I would live for a time with my uncle D. W. and his family to see if my breathing improved. It did, and even though I had never heard of Eastern New Mexico University in nearby Portales until I went to Clovis, that's where I started college in the fall of 1958.

Morris, it occurs to me, by leaving Mississippi to go to school in Texas, moved from the South properly speaking to the Southwest. So did I, with my move from Arkansas to New Mexico. And though his experiences at a large and famous school like the University of Texas were in many ways different from mine, parts of his story still resonate with me and get the memories flowing.

Morris writes eloquently of the excitement of discovering ideas, and "not of discovering *certain* books, but the simple *presence* of books." That's a bit of an exaggeration for me, as I had already learned to enjoy reading by the time I graduated from Greenwood High School in 1958 and entered Eastern New Mexico University, but I do remember the excitement of learning, about *everything*, it seems. And part of the learning for me involved being away from home; interestingly, I do not remember feeling "desperately homesick" as Morris says he did. Part of the learning also was my exposure for the first time in my life to diversity, sitting in class and living in the dormitory with African Americans, Native Americans, and Hispanic Americans. Recently, when asked to write a few memories for a book about the old rock school house in Greenwood, I mostly told fun stories, but I did say "Trying to think of anything that could have been better [about my educational experience in Greenwood], it occurs to me that DIVERSITY would have been nice—but Greenwood simply didn't have it then."

Fortunately, Mother had prepared me somewhat for the diversity I ran into at ENMU, and right away I made friends with Robert, a Black guy from Gadsden, Alabama. When the Christmas break came around, Robert and I worked out a deal where he would ride with me to Fort Smith, Arkansas, where he would catch a bus and go on to Gadsden. I had a car, and he didn't, and we figured we could share the driving, the costs (hey, gas was about 17.9 cents per gallon in those days!), and it would be more fun. As we approached Shamrock, Texas, I was getting hungry, so I started telling Robert about a café there that I liked. As I recall, he wasn't responding very enthusiastically, but I was too naive to know why. When I said, "There it is, on the right," he blurted out something like, "I don't want to go there, Davie! They probably wouldn't serve me, they probably wouldn't serve *you* if we went in there together, couldn't we eat somewhere else, please?" We drove on down the road and ate together in the car at a drive-in; by then, sensitized a bit to the issue, I noticed that we got some pretty weird stares! I was embarrassed by that whole incident, *enraged* by it. My friend Robert and I couldn't sit down together and eat a hamburger where we wanted, in our own country?! Such little incidents can make a profound difference in our lives, can't they? By the time I got to the University of Oklahoma in 1963 to begin work on my Ph.D., I was committed to and active in the civil rights movement.

Indeed, that incident probably had something to do with my becoming politicized enough that in 1960, when Edward M. Kennedy visited the ENMU campus on behalf of his brother John's Presidential campaign, I was part of the group that organized it. Bear in mind that I couldn't vote yet—I was born in 1940, and in those days, you still had to be 21. Two memories of that visit stand out. First, marching with a group of people from the dormitory to the stage we'd erected for Teddy to speak from, we sang a little campaign ditty, something like "We're marching down to Washington to shake hands with President Kennedy."

And second, while he was speaking, a dog got underneath the stage and barked persistently. He handled it well, saying at one point, "That dog must be a Republican!"

Morris got caught up in fraternity life at the University of Texas. I did not at ENMU; indeed, I can't even remember social fraternities and sororities existing there. But as a music major for my first two years before I changed to history, I did join Kappa Kappa Psi, the national honorary band fraternity, and though it did some good work, I must admit I remember some of the anti-intellectual silliness that Morris associates with fraternity life, and it was the *intellectual* stuff that was really grabbing and shaking this boy from Greenwood! Was there a course that I had to take, as a part of my first two years of general education, that I did *not* like and learn from? Some were better than others, of course, but I really don't think so; somehow I sensed even then, and I realize it all the more now, that *all* of that, even the disciplines I had no intention of pursuing further, were part of making me an educated person. Morris writes: "It took me years to understand that words are often as important as experience, because words make experience last, but here, in the spring of my freshman year, there were men who were teaching me these things, perhaps with very little hope that anyone in their classrooms remotely cared, and I think perhaps I may have been listening." So was I —what excitement!

But clearly, the discipline I got *most* excited about was history! I already had some interest in history going into college, thanks in part to Charles Martin, my high school band director, who loved to read history, and who actually gave me an original edition of the five-volume *A History of the American People* by Woodrow Wilson, which I kept until I retired in 2002, when I donated it to the East Central University library. (Along the way, of course, I had learned how deeply flawed, and racist, Woodrow Wilson's views were.) Part of my excitement about history involved a bit of disillusionment about being a music major—I began to wonder, "Do I really want to listen to 7th graders hit sour notes the rest of my life?" But more of it came from positive experiences. Dr. Ira C. Ihde taught history in a way that truly grabbed me and shook me and made me see its relevance and how exciting it could be. And he had a graduate assistant named Norman Mayhall who wrote encouraging words on the first research paper I ever wrote, including asking me if I had ever considered doing graduate work in history! As I recall, I hadn't even considered it as a major until that moment. His encouragement, my excitement over the history courses I was taking, and my doubts about a career as a band director combined to lead me to change my major to history at the end of my second year of college. I can honestly say that I have never regretted it.

I've long held that calling someone a professor suggests he/she has something to profess. I had a good friend named Harry Love who was a biology professor at East Central University. His knowledge, his insatiable intellectual curiosity, his sense of humor (known at times to be a bit rude), and most of all his passion for biology amazed me. I think he honestly couldn't understand why *everyone* wouldn't want to be a biologist. Just so, I came to feel over the years that history has that kind of draw. What could possibly be more exciting and relevant than the study of human behavior in all its rich variety, and how it has changed over time?!

But I'm getting ahead of myself here. Morris spent lots of time as an undergraduate shuttling back and forth between Texas and Mississippi. Just so, I spent a lot of time shuttling back and forth between New Mexico and Arkansas. It was on those trips that I first began to fall in love with Oklahoma. It was on one such trip, of course, one of the first, that Robert and I had our experience in Shamrock. But if Morris is being honest, he came to feel repulsion at the racist views of his hometown earlier than I did. He tells of driving home at the end of his third year in his "ramshackle Plymouth with dual exhausts" (mine was a ramshackle Ford with dual exhausts) and finding out right away that a meeting was planned to organize a local chapter of the White Citizens Council. He attended. But as the meeting proceeded, "I felt an urge to get out of there," he writes. *"Who are these people?* I asked myself. What was I doing there? Was this the kind of place I had grown up in and never wanted to leave? I knew in that instant, in the middle of a mob in our school auditorium, that a mere three years in Texas had taken me irrevocably, even without my recognizing it, from home." My process of realizing that began earlier, as I look back, in the 50s, when my Mom fortunately gave me an alternative model to the predominant racism, but it has been on-going—the most recent example a high school classmate who inexplicably began to forward his right-wing racist hate-filled diatribes to me, one of which referred to our President as "Hussein the Terrorist Sympathizer Obama." I remember thinking, as I told that classmate that I was interested in diverse views but that kind of thing was simply unacceptable, and then proceeded to add his e-mail address to the list of those to be intercepted by my Spam filter, that perhaps his views were more acceptable in Greenwood than mine....but I'm still reluctant to admit that.

"Texas, I came to feel, would never engage my whole emotional being the way Mississippi had," writes Morris, "for to live childhood and adolescence in a brooding, isolated place shapes one forever in its image, but Texas would never cease to have a hold on my imagination; it had given me a deep and liberating confirmation of values. Mississippi would lurk forever in the heart; Texas was where I reached maturity." Substitute New Mexico for Texas and Arkansas for Mississippi and that works for me.

Morris talks of the "downright prejudice" he witnessed as a part of the fraternity system at the University of Texas. It occurs to me that I didn't see that until I went to the University of Oklahoma. I remember standing side by side with my good friend Jimmie Lewis Franklin—only the second African American ever to receive a Ph.D. from OU, he went on to a distinguished career which included Vanderbilt University and the presidency of the Southern Historical Association—at a "sympathy demonstration" for the march on Selma, Alabama, in 1965, and having a frat rat wave the Confederate flag at us! It gives me some context for that to realize, as Danney Goble, one of Oklahoma's great historians, helped me to understand, that to really understand the state of Oklahoma, you need to get over its predominant Western/frontier/cowboys and Indians image and realize the extent to which Oklahoma is part of the South. As

Danney put it, "they don't call southeastern Oklahoma 'Little Dixie' for nothing."

Morris speaks of talking until midnight on one occasion after he had moved to New York with an old friend from Mississippi, and though he tries to make Mississippi sound almost unique in producing "a genuine set of exiles, almost in the European sense"—"alienated from home yet forever drawn back to it, seeking some form of personal liberty elsewhere yet obsessed with the texture and the complexity of the place from which they had departed as few Americans from other states could ever be"—I can definitely see what he means. Indeed, I'm thinking that's part of why Charles Angeletti, a life-long friend from Greenwood, Arkansas, insisted I should read *North Toward Home*!

Speaking of riding the subway to work in New York City each morning, Morris says, "In three years of waiting on this platform I had yet to hear one 'good morning' exchanged among any of my fellow passengers, for human communication was normally restricted to atavistic grumbles and more direct early-morning obscenities." Not all would agree with that as an accurate portrayal of New York, certainly, but it does remind me of why I *still* like small Southern towns—and perhaps a small part of the reason I stayed in Oklahoma after being educated there....*here*! But I have also felt what Morris describes as "the positive aspect" of the isolation of big-city Northern life: ". . . privacy . . . the inalienable right to be left alone, free of the petty inquisitiveness, the totalitarian moralities, of the American small town." *Gossip* was always one of my least favorite things about small-town Southern life (though not nearly as serious as racism, dealt with elsewhere).

Morris tells of being asked once in an interview about his Southern background, "How did you get liberated?" Taken by surprise, he blurted out, "I'm not. I'm still tryin'." Similarly, he writes of his acceptance of New York as his home, a feeling, he says, that "had been a long time in coming: you did not have to go to your sources again to survive; one's past was *inside* of a man anyway; it would remain there forever." Indeed. But Morris ends his book by recounting a trip back home to Mississippi, visiting with his Mother and Grandmother, and including the opportunity to show his son some of his roots. His conclusion: "Why was it, in such moments just before I leave the South, did I always feel some easing of a great burden? It was as if someone had taken some terrible weight off my shoulders, or as if some old grievance had suddenly fallen away. The big plane took off, and circled in widening arcs over the city, over the landmarks of my past, and my people's. Then, slowly, with a lifting heavy as steel, it circled once more, and turned north toward home."

A powerful scene in some ways. Yet. I don't have to go to the northeast, or to a big city, to go home. For me, home is northeastern Oklahoma, the small town of Spavinaw, some 70 miles northeast of Tulsa. Is it perfect? Of course not. People are not perfect, so neither are their towns. But at this late stage of life, I'm more realistic about all that. And when I come south from T General Store two miles north of town and curve down into the valley and see the welcoming trees, I know I'm almost home.

CHAPTER 4

War, Howard Zinn, and Me

I belong, I'm proud to say, to a national organization called Historians Against the War. We formed in 2003, right after the beginning of the war on Iraq. Our current Mission Statement reads:

> As historically minded activists, scholars, students, and teachers, we stand opposed to wars of aggression, military occupations of foreign lands, and imperial efforts by the United States and other powerful nations to dominate the internal life of other countries.
>
> In particular, we continue to demand a speedy end to US military involvement in Iraq, and we insist on the withdrawal, not the expansion, of US and NATO military forces in Afghanistan. We also call for a sharp reduction of US military bases overseas, and an end to US financial and military support of regimes that repress their people, or that occupy the territories of other peoples. We favor as well a drastic redirection of national resources away from military spending and toward urgently needed domestic programs.
>
> We deplore the secrecy, deception, and distortion of history, the repeated violation of international law, and the attack on civil liberties domestically that have accompanied US policies of war and militarism—policies that became especially belligerent in the aftermath of September 11.
>
> We fear that the current, rapidly escalating crisis of global capitalism, which is creating suffering worldwide, will lead to escalating wars abroad and intensifying repression at home. We support solutions to this crisis that seek to enrich the lives and increase the power of people globally, and protect their fundamental human rights. We are unalterably opposed to any attempts to solve the crisis at their expense.

> We are aware that, in the words of the late historian William Appleman Williams, "empire as a way of life" has long characterized the United States and is not easily changed. However, we are mindful as well that the current conjunction of international and domestic crises offers an opportunity to alter longstanding destructive patterns. As historians, we believe that we can and must make a contribution to the broad, international movements for peace, democracy, and environmental and social justice. In pursuing our objectives, we look toward building and joining alliances with a wide variety of intellectual and activist groups that share our concerns.

In 2006, HAW held its national meeting in Austin, at the University of Texas. I was honored to be asked to introduce Howard Zinn as the feature speaker. This event was in the LBJ Auditorium, and I will never forget the overflow crowd—and the irony of hearing Zinn talk about LBJ's lies about Vietnam in the LBJ Auditorium!

The 2008 national meeting was in Atlanta. I chaired a session on Zinn's life and work. The paper I presented follows.

☮

Some of my earliest memories of "historical events" are of war, specifically World War II. I was born in the summer of 1940. I *think* I remember the death of FDR. Neither "president" nor "death" means much to a 4-year-old, but it seems to me I remember everybody being really upset and sad. I'm even more confident that I remember the end of the war—though mostly what I remember is personalizing it to "Alright, my uncles D. W. and Harvey are coming home!" Uncle D. W. was one of my favorites, but he was on "clean-up squads" in Europe at the end of the war, and spent the rest of his life in and out of veterans' hospitals with "nervous breakdowns." Wars do that kind of thing to people, don't they? I should also mention that World War II deeply impacted my life far too early for me to remember—just a few months after I was born in western Arkansas, the government came in and bought out all the family farms in the area to turn it into Fort Chaffee. Wars do *that* kind of thing to people, too, don't they?

Perhaps you can see already that this is not a "traditional scholarly paper." But then I assumed when I submitted my proposal that this would not be a traditional scholarly history conference, either, among other reasons because of the focus and distinct point of view suggested by the title ("U. S. Empire"?!), the words "and Activists" included in the sub-title, and the group sponsoring it, Historians Against the War. Instead, what I attempt here is a personal essay dealing with myself in relation to war—both war in general, and specifically World War II, Vietnam, and Iraq—and the influence Howard Zinn has had on me in this area.

One thing further about World War II. I've been reading *A Strong West Wind*, a memoir by Gail Caldwell. She writes "Our dads were heroes—all of them were heroes, it seemed—and it was our tender burden to be the little soldiers who made it all worthwhile."[1] Even though my Dad was *not* a war hero—flat feet, if I remember correctly, kept him from enlisting, and I always felt he regretted he had been unable to serve like his brothers—I can identify with what Caldwell writes. It seems, looking back on it now, that I grew up assuming that the only thing to do when your country went to war was support it. It's not that I thought *not* supporting it was unpatriotic or something, it's just that other options never occurred to me, were not a part of my experience.

Fast forward through the Korean War. Sorry, but I was in about the 4th-5th-6th grades during those years, and I honestly don't remember the war penetrating my consciousness at that time!

But broader historical events, including the civil rights movement, certainly *had* penetrated my consciousness by 1963, when I enrolled in the Ph.D. program in history at the University of Oklahoma. My undergraduate years had been spent at Eastern New Mexico University, where, for the first time in my life, I sat side by side in classrooms with African Americans, Native Americans, and Hispanic Americans. It was all a revelation for a boy from Greenwood, Arkansas, where there were no Black students, I heard the n-word a lot, etc. At Oklahoma, I was involved in several demonstrations over the next three years—to support national events like the Selma march, to integrate some local facilities that were still running behind, that kind of thing. One of my good friends in those days, a good friend still, was one of the first African Americans to receive a Ph.D. from the University of Oklahoma. I *think* it was during those years that I first heard of the work of Howard Zinn, specifically his books related to the South and the civil rights movement, *The Southern Mystique* and *SNCC: The New Abolitionists*, both published in 1964.

I *know* that the first book of Zinn's that I read was *Vietnam: The Logic of Withdrawal*. It came out in 1967, by which time I was a young Assistant Professor of History at the University of Tulsa. What can I say? It was a *revelation* for me! Oh, I had, of course, as a serious student of history, learned by that time that there had been people who spoke out against *all* the wars in our history. And I had already begun to doubt that what we were doing in Vietnam made sense, and I had certainly begun to doubt that our government was telling us the truth about it. But I've mentioned my background, so it should not surprise you when I say that I felt kind of guilty for having those kind of doubts. Zinn's book helped me get over that—and more.

There's no need for me to summarize the entire book here. Suffice it to say that Zinn made the case in powerful and unique ways that what we needed to do in Vietnam was to get the heck out! He looked at the war from a *Japanese* perspective first. He talked about traveling there and finding the Japanese people "virtually unanimous in their belief that United States policy in Vietnam was not just a bit awry, but profoundly wrong." Some, he reported, were even willing to say "You are behaving in Asia as we once did."

After that, Zinn turned to illuminating "A View from Within: The Negro." Noting that African Americans had largely supported World War II because of its strong element of antiracism, he then insisted that it was fundamentally different in Vietnam: "The foe is not an Anglo-Saxon racist but a mass of poor, dark-skinned peasants who resemble in many aspects of their lives the Negroes of the American rural South." The charge most often flung at the Johnson administration by blacks in connection with Vietnam was summed up in a single word: hypocrisy. (Some of you might recall the title of a movie about the extensive yet problematic involvement of blacks in Vietnam: *No Vietnamese Ever Called Me Nigger.*)

Next, Zinn turned to a chapter entitled "The View from History: What Nation Can Be Trusted?" Not surprisingly, his fundamental answer was *none*. The United States, he concluded, "must be included as a nation which, like the others, will use any means to gain its ends." Even more powerfully—realize that, when reading all this, I'm a young assistant professor of history who has not been introduced to this approach to history!—he concluded that whereas in World War II the bombing deaths of civilians resulted from "terrible mistake[s] in judgment," "*In Vietnam, . . . the bombing and shelling of civilians constitutes the war.*"

The last chapter of *Vietnam: The Logic of Withdrawal* was entitled "A Speech for LBJ." It was *brilliant*. But it is not unfair to suggest that it is also a perfect illustration of just how far from mainstream historical writing Zinn was, in terms of both methodology and what he has Johnson say, which was essentially all the arguments we have summarized here, and the conclusion: "My fellow Americans [*That* certainly sounds like LBJ, doesn't it?!], good night and sleep well. We are no longer at war in Vietnam."[2]

One group of people was so impressed by Zinn's book that they secured permission from Beacon Press, the publisher, to run the imaginary LBJ speech as an ad in the *New York Times*. And *I* was so impressed that I began a short time thereafter to speak out against the war myself. To do so in Tulsa, Oklahoma, was quite unpopular at that time. The University of Tulsa has a Presbyterian background and is deeply connected to/supported by oil wealth, Tulsa itself has sometimes been called the Buckle of the Bible Belt (think Oral Roberts, among others), and Oklahoma has not even voted Democratic in a Presidential election since 1964 and is one of the reddest of the red states in today's terminology. But I felt comfortable with what I was doing —even though I paid a price for it, both professionally (I was denied a promotion I clearly deserved on a strictly professional basis in about 1973) and personally (I remember friends *uninviting* me to dinner on one occasion after reading about an anti-war speech I had given in the local press, and on one sad occasion my sister actually blamed my radical political activity for some health problems our parents were having). Thanks in large part to

Howard Zinn, I had reached the point of believing that history and common sense supported the anti-war position, and that believing that, it was not only okay but a moral imperative for me to speak out. I remember giving an "anti-inaugural address" the day Nixon took over in 1973, which I ended with the upraised fist and the words "Power to the People!"

I was influenced by not just the anti-Vietnam War movement, but by all the major movements of the 60s. Zinn helped again. The next book of his that I read was *The Politics of History*, published in 1970. Again, *revelation* is not too strong a word. Just look at the title, and think of the largely traditional education I had experienced. *History* is *political?*! I mentioned the other movements of the 60s, by which I mean the civil rights movement, the movement for women's equality, and the environmental movement. Over the next few years, I was influenced by/involved in all those movements. And, *a la Zinn*, developed courses that dealt with each of those subjects, refusing to compartmentalize the professional and the personal. I taught many times a course on American Radical Thought, which included pacifism, non-violence, and specific anti-war movements. I taught with a colleague the first African American history course ever offered at the University of Tulsa. I taught courses on Women in American History. And I taught American Environmental History, in which I tried to trace the relationship between humans and their environment here in the United States, including our use and abuse of natural resources and our belated efforts to clean up our environment and preserve some of our natural beauty. I always presented the Native American approach to the natural environment as an alternative model. And, since I've already shown I'm not hesitant to reveal embarrassing things in order to make a point: I remember wearing a tie-dyed t-shirt that among other things responded to the right's "America—Love It or Leave It" slogan by saying "Earth—Love It or Leave It!"

Howard Zinn, then, not only helped me develop my anti-war beliefs and practices, he also, more broadly, influenced my approach to history. Objectivity is a myth, neither possible nor desirable. Look out most of all for those who claim to be completely objective. To the extent they succeed, they do a history which helps to prop up the status quo—and what could possibly be more political than that?! Instead, we should be as open and honest and up front about our biases as possible, and then proceed to write the very best history we can, being true, of course, to the sources, but also being true to the present and its concerns. The past for the past's sake? The past doesn't have a sake; it is past. We study the past to learn about the present—and to influence the future. And hopefully by doing history this way we contribute in some small way to the on-going struggle for peace and justice.

Zinn's most famous work, of course, his *magnum opus*, so to speak, is *A People's History of the United States*, originally published in 1980. It has gone through several editions since then, and has sold well over a million copies. I don't have time to say much about it here, and probably don't need to. Suffice it to say that it looks at our history from the standpoint of the dispossessed. It is, as the famous phrase from the 60s goes, history "from the bottom up." It is also history from the outside in, for Zinn's heroes and heroines tend to be those who fought for peace and justice and equality—those, in short, who took seriously the words of the Declaration of Independence and led movements to try to turn those ideals into reality for all Americans. I have been so influenced by that approach to history that it not only describes my methods for the rest of my career in my U. S. history courses, I have also tried to apply it to Oklahoma history, in my courses, and in two collections of "alternative views" of Oklahoma history which emphasize women, minorities, common people, and radicals who worked to improve the quality of the lives of all the people.[3]

But I need to move to the current "war on terror," and specifically Iraq. I knew from the beginning, the morning of 9/11 as I sat watching in shock the events of that terrible day unfold, that I could not support a war-like response. That view was reenforced when I dealt with the events in my classes that day, and one young man clearly thought the proper response was to start killing "A-rabs." But I also needed to turn to Howard

Zinn to help me clarify/refine/support my views. Once again, he did not let me down.

When I approached Zinn to ask him if he would cooperate with me in my research on a book on his life and writings—by granting me interviews and access to his papers, and by responding to e-mail queries—he said ". . . . of course I'll cooperate. Otherwise, I will appear in your book not only as a radical but as a surly one." I've never run into anyone, even among those who differ with Zinn, who consider him surly. He cooperated fully. And when I contacted him as part of my preparation for this presentation, he emphasized two things: *The Zinn Reader*, which was published in 1997 so that I had already had the opportunity to use it in the research for my book, published in 2003; and *A Power Governments Cannot Suppress*, published in 2007 and Zinn's newest (so far as I know—even in his mid-80s, it's hard to keep up with him!), which I was aware of but had not yet had the opportunity to read. I have read it now, and it speaks powerfully to some of the issues I am trying to address here. First, the title: "a power governments cannot suppress," it occurs to me, is close to the heart of his work. Clearly, Zinn believes, and so, most of the time, do I, that we the people do indeed have the power, a power governments cannot suppress, and that we have used it and must continue to use it to move things slowly along the road toward justice and peace.

Pardon me for stringing together some brief quotes from *A Power Governments Cannot Suppress*—Zinn has always spoken best for himself. As far as I know, his first published response to the events of 9/11 appeared in the September 28, 2001, issue of the *Chronicle of Higher Education*. The essay shows Zinn calling passionately and eloquently for "Compassion, Not Vengeance." The images on television, he said, were indeed "heart-breaking," but "then our political leaders came on television, and I was horrified and sickened again." For they spoke of retaliation, vengeance, punishment, war. "And I thought: They have learned nothing, absolutely nothing, from the history of the 20th century. . . . We need to think about the resentment all over the world felt by people who have been the victims of American military action. . . . We need to decide that we will not go to war, whatever reason is conjured up by the politicians, because war in our time is always indiscriminate, a war against innocents, a war against children. War is terrorism, magnified a hundred times." Zinn concluded: "Our security can only come by using our national wealth, not for guns, planes, and bombs, but for the health and welfare of our people, and for people suffering in other countries. Our first thoughts should be not of vengeance, but of compassion, not of violence, but of healing."[4]

In the first chapter of *A Power Governments Cannot Suppress*, Zinn speaks more broadly of the contribution history can make. "America's future is linked to how we understand our past," he begins. "For this reason, writing about history, for me, is never a neutral act. By writing, I hope to awaken a great consciousness of racial injustice, sexual bias, class inequality, and national hubris. . . . I write in order to illustrate the creative power of people struggling for a better world. People, when organized, have enormous power, more than any government. . . . History can tell how often governments have lied to us, how they have ordered whole populations to be massacred, how they deny the existence of the poor, how they have led us to our current historical moment—the 'Long War,' the war without end. . . . We live in a beautiful country. But people who have no respect for human life, freedom, or justice have taken it over. It is now up to all of us to take it back."[5]

One of the accusations I sometimes run into in my part of the country when I express my anti-war views is that I am being "unpatriotic." Zinn helps me understand patriotism as well. "If patriotism means supporting your government's policies without question, then we are on our way to a totalitarian state. . . . [T]rue patriotism [on the other hand] lies in supporting the values the country is supposed to cherish: equality, life, liberty, the pursuit of happiness. When our government compromises, undermines, or attacks those values, it is being unpatriotic."[6] Nationalism often goes hand in hand with patriotism. "Is not nationalism [asks Zinn—defined as] —that devotion to a flag, an anthem, a boundary, so fierce it engenders mass murder—one of the great evils of our time, along with racism and religious hatred?"[7]

Just one of Zinn's concerns in relation to the current "war on terror" is the "war" on our civil liberties. "The question is, whether Americans will at some point begin to understand that the 'war on terror' has also become a war against the liberties of Americans, and will demand that these liberties be restored. Without the right to speak freely, to dissent, we cannot evaluate what the government is doing, and so we may be swept into foreign policy adventures with no oppositional voices and later lament our silence."[8]

Though he had earlier been hesitant to call himself a pacifist, because it seemed too "absolute," Zinn writes here, in an essay entitled "The Enemy Is War," that "We must recognize that we cannot depend on the governments of the world to abolish war, therefore, we, the people of the world, must take up the challenge." Zinn believes "there is one crucial fact which gives us enormous power: the governments of the world cannot wage war without the participation of the people." The conclusion of that essay is this: "The abolition of war has become not only desirable but necessary if the planet is to be saved. It is an idea whose time has come."[9]

A central theme of Zinn's work that has always impressed me is his optimism. The final chapter of *A Power Governments Cannot Suppress* reminds us again of his brand of optimism; it is called "The Optimism of Uncertainty." "I am totally confident not that the world will get better, but that we should not give up the game before all the cards have been played." "I try hard to match my friends in their pessimism about the world (is it just my friends?)," he writes, "but I keep encountering people, who in spite of all the evidence of terrible things happening everywhere, give me hope." Looking at history also gives him hope. An optimist, he insists, "isn't necessarily a blithe, slightly sappy whistler in the dark of our time. To be hopeful in bad times is not being foolishly romantic. It is based on the fact that human history is a history not only of competition and cruelty but also of compassion, sacrifice, courage, kindness." Besides, "The future is an infinite succession of presents, and to live now as we think human beings should live, in defiance of all that is bad around us, is itself a marvelous victory."[10]

Just one more quote: "Education can, and should, be dangerous to the existing social structure."[11] But enough with the quotations already! Let me use those words of Zinn to lead into a few concluding thoughts of my own. *This* quote is from my book on Zinn:

> [Zinn] has played, for virtually his entire adult life, the role that radicals have always played historically. They are always out there—outside the mainstream, redefining the mainstream— raising the hard questions, pulling the rest of society along, sometimes kicking and screaming. The abolitionists of the 1830s and the women's rights advocates of the 1840s are just the two most obvious examples from American history. Even those who do not define themselves as radical, by very definition the majority of any given group of people, can usually be brought to acknowledge the important role radicals play, the changes they help bring about from which all people eventually benefit. It can even be argued, without doing violence to the definition of any of the terms, that Zinn is a radical/patriot/historian. For radical suggests getting to the root of something; and patriot means of our fathers, thus suggesting getting back to the basic principles, for example, the Declaration of Independence, upon which this country was founded; and history has as one of its root words, historia, to inquire—no limits, to inquire! Zinn's inquiry has left us a legacy that respects all people, that insists all people are a part of history, not just the presidents and kings and queens and generals and the rich. If his focus has often been on the common people, and even more on those who have worked to bring about fundamental change, that is simply because those people were for so long excluded from history (or ridiculed when included).[12]

I entitled my study of Zinn's life and writings *Howard Zinn: A Radical American Vision*. That sub-title seems relevant here:

> [Zinn's work] is radical because it seeks to bring about fundamental change in the political, social, economic order, to get to the roots.
>
> It is American because it is firmly grounded in the ideals on which the United States of America was founded, the ideals of the Declaration of Independence, such ideals as life and liberty and the pursuit of happiness and equality and self-determination that are so self-evident and inherent that no government has the right to take them away; much of Zinn's version of American history is the story of a continuing effort, still by no means complete, to live up to those ideals in reality. When David Barsamian asked Zinn a question about "left values," the first thing he thought of was socialism. Left values, he insisted, were egalitarian values. "If I had to say what is at the center of left

values, it's the idea that everyone has a fundamental right to the necessary things of life and the good things of life, that there should be no disproportions in the world." But Zinn also thought of the Declaration of Independence. "The principles of the Declaration of Independence—even though it was not written by a leftist—Thomas Jefferson, a leftist?—the idea that everybody has an equal right to life, liberty, and the pursuit of happiness, to me is a remarkable statement of left values."

Finally, it is a vision because indeed it is not yet a reality but a hope. But visions do not become reality through mere hope. Much work is required. Howard Zinn has done his share.[13]

Now, let us do our share! In short, what have I learned from Howard Zinn, my study of history, and my experience that is relevant for our current situation, for this seemingly endless war, for this conference? Just this: We live in a world in which war is never the best solution to a problem. And to say that—in general, and now about what we are doing in Iraq in particular—is deeply moral, even patriotic.

---

1 Gail Caldwell, *A Strong West Wind* (New York: Random House, 2006), p. 9.

2 Howard Zinn, *Vietnam: The Logic of Withdrawal* (Boston: Beacon Press, 1967), spread out from pages 9 through 125.

3 The two volumes I have edited are *"An Oklahoma I Had Never Seen Before:" Alternative Views of Oklahoma History* (Norman: University of Oklahoma Press, 1994), and *Alternative Oklahoma: Contrarian Views of the Sooner State* (Norman: University of Oklahoma Press, 2007). Zinn has been kind enough to praise both volumes, and even to say that he hopes they become a model for similar works on other states.

4 Davis D. Joyce, *Howard Zinn: A Radical American Vision* (Amherst, New York: Prometheus Books, 2003), p. 220. Parts of the *Chronicle* piece also appear in *A Power Governments Cannot Suppress*.

5 Howard Zinn, *A Power Governments Cannot Suppress* (San Francisco: City Lights Books, 2007), pp. 11-16.

6 *Ibid.*, pp. 111-112.

7 *Ibid.*, p. 143.

8 *Ibid.*, p. 172.

9 *Ibid.*, pp. 189 and 197.

10 *Ibid.*, pp. 267-270.

11 *Ibid.*, p. 230.

12 Joyce, *Howard Zinn: A Radical American Vision*, p. 253.

13 *Ibid.*, pp. 251-252.

CHAPTER 5

Teaching American History Abroad

I have long believed that one does not really *learn* a subject until he or she begins to try to *teach* it. Just so, my experience teaching abroad led me to the realization that one does not really learn American history until he or she tries to teach it to non-Americans. I was fortunate to have the experience of teaching abroad twice—once, for a semester, in 1981, at the University of Keele in England, and the other time for two years, 1994-1996, at Kossuth University in Debrecen, Hungary. (Later, it was renamed the University of Debrecen.)

When I secured the opportunity to go to England to teach, the *Tulsa Tribune* (a newspaper now defunct, like so many others), ran a feature story on June 17, 1981, under the headline "TU [i. e., University of Tulsa] historian to teach the English a thing or two." Rather embarrassing. But in the story, Emily Parish quoted me as saying "I've said I'm going to teach them the truth about the American Revolution," but then she added, "Joyce said jokingly." She quoted me saying further, "Of course, with that attitude, I may go over there and not make it back." In reality, as I recall, "the truth" about the American Revolution is simply seen differently by Americans and Englishmen—as is so often the case with history. Many of my students at Keele seemed rather disinterested in the American Revolution, seeing it as a relatively minor episode in the long history of the decline of the British Empire; we Americans, of course, see it as the very origin of our country!

Parish was kind enough to suggest, spinning off from my comment about "attitude," that "In fact, Joyce's 'attitude' probably will draw students to him at Keele, as it has students at TU."

Relevant for seeing history differently, she noted my specialization in historiography, the study of historians and their interpretations of history. "Joyce quickly emphasized," she wrote, "that there is not one, true story of how the 'Great Republic,' as Winston Churchill once dubbed it, came about." She quoted me: "Too often, history courses are presented with the idea that 'These are the facts of history.' In the stereotypical history class, students receive a textbook and a professor, and that's it. But that's not enough. You must show that different historians in different ages see history in different ways." I used the American Revolution as a case study of how historical interpretations change not only over time, but also are dependent on one's climate of opinion, that is to say on their age/gender/ethnicity/ ideology....and many other factors. "If you don't teach all views, you're deceiving the student into thinking there's only one, and that's just not so," I concluded. That was some 30 years ago as I write this, and I still contend that is indeed the case.

When Carole and I learned we were going to get to go to England for the first time in our lives (indeed, the *Tribune* noted that I had never been abroad before), we were very excited. Noting that we were going to take the luxury liner *Queen Elizabeth II* as our means of travel, the paper, rather embarrassingly, quoted me as saying, "We had to take out a loan to do it, but we figured it could be the only time we'll ever have this chance."

Fortunately, we were to have another chance to travel abroad to teach—but a bit more about England first. My notes from that experience remind me that when I was given the opportunity to present a lecture as part of the seminar series put on by the David Bruce Centre for American Studies at Keele University, I chose as my topic "The New Left in American History," reflective of both my historiographical orientation and my leftward leanings. I had just recently read Howard Zinn's *A People's History of the United States*, which had been published in 1980, and was making extensive use of it in my teaching, as I had already been influenced by Zinn's earlier works, *Vietnam: The Logic of Withdrawal* and *The Politics of History*. So it seemed natural for me to talk about Zinn and other important "radical" or "new left" historians such as William Appleman Williams, Staughton Lynd, and Eugene Genovese. (Also, I was then at work on my revision of the Michael Kraus work on American historiography, *The Writing of American History*, and one of the new chapters I contributed dealt with those "conflict" historians of the 1960s.) I remember being surprised in the question and answer session that followed my lecture that one of my faculty colleagues in American Studies—indeed, in history specifically—asked a question about why Zinn was so "negative" in his view of American history. I was surprised, because to me Zinn was *not* negative in his approach, but rather very positive in his optimistic conclusion that "We, the People" had successfully organized and brought about change in the past (think abolition of slavery, enfranchisement of women, on and on) and therefore could do so in the future as well.

Upon my return from England, both the *Tribune* and the *Tulsa World* carried articles about my experience; it's fun to read them after all these years and allow them to remind me of more memories that seem to be relevant here. The *Tribune* piece, by J. B. Carlile this time, ran under the headline, "TU Professor Finds British Speak Different English Language." "Even though we speak the same language, you don't forget you're a foreigner," Carlile quotes me as saying. That is indeed true! One of my favorite examples involved seeing a sign in front of a restaurant on the motorway (we'd say "interstate") that read, "No Football Coaches Allowed." In small print, underneath, it said, "without prior arrangements." At first, I couldn't imagine what it meant. What, I wondered, do they have against Bud Wilkinson or Bear Bryant? But of course "football" meant what we Americans call soccer. (My friend Tibor in Hungary once informed me that "What you Americans call soccer, the rest of the world calls football, and what you Americans call football, the rest of the world doesn't care much about.") And "coach" meant "bus." So the meaning? No bus loads of soccer fans could go thronging into that restaurant without letting them know ahead of time that they were coming! Another example I recall is that Carole and I were in London, walking a great deal and seeing the sights, and we decided it was time to take an underground train, what we would call a subway, back to where we were staying, so when we saw a sign that read "Subway," we headed down the stairs. We found ourselves going through a tunnel....and coming *up* the stairs on the other side! We looked at each other in amazement for a minute before realizing that a "subway" was a safe way of walking underneath a busy street, and what we were looking for was indeed the "Underground"! Just one more, more directly relevant for my teaching. I was lecturing about Jacksonian Democracy. Thinking a physical description of Jackson was relevant, with his frontiersman image being part of the phenomenon, I said he was "6 feet, 1 inch tall, and weighed about 140 pounds." I remember noticing some confused looks and uncomfortable giggles, so I asked why. Turns out, you can start an argument even among English folks about how they measure height, though most of my contacts agree it's in feet and inches. But they definitely state weight differently: Apparently, since fourteen pounds equals one "stone," I should have said Jackson weighed "ten stone."

There's also a memory of that same fall London visit—to see the important radical rock and roll band, The Clash, by the way, live at the Lyceum!—which involves one of the few times I remember being embarrassed to be abroad and be American. President Reagan had just said something about the "acceptability" of limited nuclear war. Western Europeans figured that meant he considered it acceptable for *them* to be in the area affected. Millions of Englishmen took to the streets of London in protest that weekend. Carole and I tried most of the time to keep our Okie American accents quiet on that visit!

I talked a lot in the *Tribune* piece about how my experience was a "broadening" one. "I had to think about their point of view, especially when teaching about the American Revolution," I said—more realistically than my comments on that subject *before* crossing the Atlantic! "I couldn't say 'us' and mean Americans." I found teaching in an "American Studies" program, as opposed to a history department, itself to be broadening, requiring as it did an interdisciplinary approach, working with colleagues in literature, political science, geography. I also found things such as class size and attendance requirements to be eye-opening. Students were required to attend small group (usually six, as I recall) discussions, but *not* required to attend the related lectures. As a write that, I must confess that I still find that rather strange. But I enjoyed the small group discussions immensely, and found it gave me an opportunity to get to know individual students better. Because students took only two classes per nine-week term, they were expected to do a lot of outside reading, and most of them did.

The *Tulsa World* article, by Ron Wolfe, appeared under the headline "1776, and all that," with the sub-heading "Teaching history in England not all beer and skittles." Both papers, by the way, ran their coverage on the same day, January 21, 1982, and both were quite similar in content. Wolfe was, however, impressed by my attraction to those "warm, friendly, almost family-type places," the English pubs. "And anyone who says English beer tastes bad and comes served hot just hasn't made a proper, scholarly study of the subject, Joyce argues. 'They don't serve it hot. It's pleasantly cool,' he said. 'They just don't freeze the taste out of it.'" I was not as impressed with the English standard steak and kidney pie. Wolfe noted correctly that I would be "just as happy not to see another steak and kidney pie." I did, however, in my defense, learn to love fish and chips!

As I make the transition to sharing some reflections on teaching American history in Hungary, let me first note some things the English and Hungarian experiences had in common. First, I'd say emphatically that I learned at least as much as I taught. That's what I meant when I talked about my English experience being a "broadening" one. Also in both countries, admission standards were higher, with only the elite among high school graduates (about 10% in Hungary, as I recall) getting into higher education. That had its advantages, of course; I rarely had a "bad" student in either country, and only remember having one "discipline" problem in Hungary and absolutely none in England. The *World* quoted me saying on this subject, "They're far more selective, and getting more so. Our system may let in people who are not good students, but I like it better. It's more democratic." I still feel that way. I had "readjustment" problems to a certain extent after both my English and Hungarian experiences. But I remember them being worse after I returned to East Central University from Hungary, perhaps in part because I was there so much longer, two years. In any case, Carole could tell you that I almost drove her crazy my first semester back, coming home complaining about "bad" students who didn't do the reading, who constantly caused disruption in the classroom, etc. The English students, I'd say, showed some knowledge of American history, but from a different perspective, while the Hungarian students in general showed less knowledge but a higher level of interest. (I remember once, in Hungary, thinking I was giving a brilliant lecture on the coming of the American Revolution, and talking specifically at some length about the role played in that process by the Molasses Act. A hand went up. I called on the young man. He asked, "What is the meaning of that word, 'molasses'?")

Though not directly related to the specifically academic portion of our experience abroad, I cannot resist the temptation to make brief comments about the fact that Carole and I experienced "socialized medicine" in both countries—and loved it! What it means is that your tax burden may be a bit higher, but your basic health care needs are cared for. What's wrong with that?! My hope, as I write this, is that the recently-passed health care reforms of the Obama administration will help to improve our system here in the United States, where we have long had one of the highest quality health care systems in the world but one of the least accessible/affordable.

Which brings us to Hungary. Allow me to begin by saying I loved Hungary! I loved the people, the food, the drink, the culture, almost everything about the experience. Carole and I were there long enough, two years, that we got over feeling like tourists, and felt in many ways that we actually belonged. I still maintain close ties with numerous Hungarian friends. (I should note, in all fairness, that I'm not contrasting Hungary with England here to make England look bad, and that I still have good English friends as well, including Martin Crawford, a faculty colleague while I was there, now retired, and Mark Jancovich, one of my students while there, now a faculty member at the University of East Anglia. Both helped me—sort of—to make sense of Andrew Jackson's height and weight! As did good friend Stephen Saunders of Tulsa, former English citizen, now an American, who even called his Mum and Dad for consultation!) My first Hungarian friend, indeed the first Hungarian person I ever met that I'm aware of, was Tamas Vrauko. Marvin Kroeker, a good friend and colleague at East Central University, and I directed a National Endowment for the Humanities Summer Seminar for School Teachers there in 1990; Tamas (or "Tom the Hun," as he wrote on the coffee cup he used that summer) was one of the international participants. Thanks to my continuing contact with him, I learned that Kossuth University was looking for someone to appoint to a two-year term as Soros Professor of American Studies in their Institute of English and American Studies beginning in the fall of 1994. I applied, and secured the position. (By the way, for the interested reader, the "Soros" of the position title was George Soros, the Hungarian-American multi-millionaire and supporter of liberal political causes.) Before going to Hungary to begin the job, we met another Hungarian. Reading the *Ada Evening News*, we saw that there was a Hungarian exchange student, a young man named Csaba Kohegyi, graduating from nearby Calvin High School. We called the family he was staying with, and they invited us out to meet him. He gave us our first little Hungarian/ English dictionary, and we are still friends.

Dr. Bill Cole, President of East Central, was quoted in the local press as saying "ECU is implementing a much more international focus in preparing students for the future." Perhaps that attitude helped to explain why the university cooperated with me in taking a 2-year leave, rather unusual in the academic world. I claimed in that same article that my experience would ultimately benefit ECU students, and I believe it did. Also: "I think this is an exciting time to be a part of higher education in Hungary. Hungary has only been free of Communist domination for the past four or five years. The new openness has fostered a keen interest in democracy and anything North American."

Kossuth University at that time had about 6,000 students; some 500 of them were enrolled in the Institute of English and American Studies.

The Bridge, a newsletter of the Institute, also did a piece before my arrival, based on an interview I did when I was in Debrecen as a candidate for the position in April. Asked if I had ever been in Hungary before, I replied no, and that I'd only met one Hungarian person before, Tamas Vrauko. Katalin Lustyik, one of two student editors of the publication, asked me if I had ever taught outside the US, and of course I mentioned Keele. I expected Kossuth to be "a bit more difficult," I noted, in part because "I don't understand a word here. I hope I will learn the basic words." I tried! When Katalin asked me what courses I taught at ECU, I gave her my basic fields: Pre-Civil War US, American Historiography, and Oklahoma History. When she asked what courses I would teach at Kossuth, I mentioned Introduction to the Culture of the USA, Topics in American Social Phenomena, The Sociology of American Culture After World War II, and Main Currents in American Thought. Even from that list, you can see that an American scholar teaching abroad is expected to be a generalist, to say the least, and the fact is, I taught all those courses—and more!

Cherity Harris was the editor of the *ECU Journal* the first year I was away from East Central. She had a very international perspective on things, writing in an editorial shortly after the Oklahoma City bombing, which occurred while Carole and I were in Hungary obviously, that "It is time that the nation realizes that 'our people' are not just Americans. 'Our people' includes every man, woman and child everywhere." Probably because of this orientation, Cherity invited me to send "reports" to her occasionally; a couple of them appeared in the "Letters to the Editor" section. In one, I talked about some preliminary impressions of Hungarian history and national character; perhaps it bears quoting at length.

☮

I'm writing this on March 15, which is a national holiday in Hungary in honor of the revolution of 1848, led by Louis Kossuth, for whom the university where I'm teaching is named.

That revolution failed. So did the one against the Soviet Union in 1956, for which there is also a national holiday. And the greatest battle, perhaps, in Hungarian history was fought against the Turks at Mohacs in 1526. And lost. All that led me to attempt some brief, preliminary observations on the Hungarian character.

Obviously, a country with those experiences would have a fundamentally different psychology from the U. S., where we have a history of success and seem to have difficulty admitting to those occasions where we do fail (with Vietnam as the most recent example). There are no pretensions here about being the greatest country in the world; I find that refreshing. But there is a rich tradition—Hungary has been a country for about 2,000 years, (pause, as an American, to think about that)—and great pride, even as Hungary struggles to adjust to the new realities politically and economically since the end of Soviet domination.

Hungary was recently "honored" as the world's most pessimistic country, based on a poll of countries around the world in which people were asked whether they thought things would be better or worse the next year. But my Hungarian friends have convinced me that that's just realism, honesty, bluntness. Economically, certainly, things are getting worse right now.

In a discussion of why they were interested in studying about the U. S., one of my students said, "You need to realize this is Hungary, and in Hungary nothing works"—but some of his fellow students differed with him strongly and were aware that some things don't work real well in America either (try, for starters, expensive, inaccessible health care and out-of-control violence).

I've been asked a number of times whether Hungarians are friendly. It depends on what you mean. If you got on a bus around Debrecen, you'd see mostly pretty serious, somber, even glum-looking people and almost none of the surface friendliness we expect in America ("Hi, how're you doing," when we really don't want to know), and you'd conclude perhaps that Hungarians aren't very friendly. But if you stuck around a little longer, you'd learn that if by friendly you mean whether someone is there to help you solve a problem when you've got one, they're incredibly friendly. "Hungarian hospitality" is much-vaunted and very real. We have trouble buying tickets for events here—people want to give them to us. When we come home from a trip, our next-door neighbor has dinner ready for us. We went on a trip recently with one of my students; we'd never met his family, but he insisted we stay with them, and they made us feel perfectly comfortable (even though they couldn't speak a word of English!).

Part of making us feel comfortable, by the way, involved having Pepsi Cola in the house, because my student had told them that's what Carole drank!

☮

I did another column for the *Journal* on May 4, 1995—the same issue, by the way, in which Cherity Harris defined "our people" with moving broadness—and this time focused on education. I noted that students in Hungary take a heavy load (as many as 35 contact hours per week), that they have to take state exams to get into university, and that only a minority make it, and that those who do get paid for their five years of university work (yes, five years, not four) and tend to take their education very seriously.

Once again, extensive quotation seems appropriate . . .

☮

The *motivation* for university education must be different here, I am beginning to learn. For one thing, you know, I am sure, that the statistics in our own country show clearly the financial advantage a university degree gives you over the course of a lifetime. The rector of Kossuth University told me that is *not* true here in Hungary, though I have not seen statistics on it yet. But on a related point, a colleague has told me the percentage of students in Hungary trying to get into university is going up, and one of the reasons seems to be that, though they don't get paid *much* for being a student, at least they do get paid, and it's better than joining the ranks of the unemployed, which is a likely prospect considering the country's economic difficulties right now.

This may sound familiar: Higher education is in trouble financially here. The government has recently proposed a 5% cut for next year, and this in a country where university professors' salaries are already so low that many of them work additional jobs just to get by.

Along with the 5% cut, the government has proposed that students begin to pay tuition. Just 2,000 Forints a month (less than $20), but that's a lot here, and besides it is the principle of the thing, isn't it? Students know that once tuition is begun, it can only go up. There was a *massive* demonstration against these government proposals on campus about two weeks ago. Interestingly, the rector himself was among those who participated.

But away from finances for a couple of closing thoughts. Anyone who knows me knows that I encourage class discussion. My students have good English skills, but getting them to talk in class has been harder than pulling teeth. Reasons may vary, and perhaps include lack of confidence in their English in the presence of a native speaker, but colleagues have helped me understand that the main reason is probably the absence of a tradition of students speaking up in class, especially in a way that might seem to question or challenge the professor. That's a degree of authority I'm not comfortable with!

☮

Though remember that I wished my American students had been a bit *more* respectful of my authority my first semester back!

Carole had the opportunity to teach while we were in Hungary as well—a course in Conversational English for economics students at the Agricultural University in Debrecen. Her notes reminded me that we gave guest lectures for each other, me talking about 1960s rock and roll (logical since I was teaching a class on Rock Music and American Culture), and she talking about "HIV/AIDS: Testing, Counseling, and Support Groups" for my "Sociological Issues in Recent U. S. Society" course (also logical since that was an area of considerable expertise and activism for her).

I've mentioned *The Bridge*. The paper paid lots of attention to me during the two years I was there, perhaps in part because I was the first person to be Soros Professor of American Studies. Vol. 2, No. 3, November 16, 1994, featured "English Majors' Week," so I was asked to write a column, which I called "Connections." I hope you'll agree that it is worth including here in its entirety:

☮

Well into my third month in Hungary now, I've been thinking a lot about connections. Connections between people. Connections between people and the Earth.

Some readers will know that I am here partly because of a connection—with Tamas Vrauko, a graduate of Kossuth who studied with me in Oklahoma in 1990. That seminar included environmental concerns—connections with the land. The other international participant that summer was Abdoul Wahab Coulibaly, from the West African nation of Mali. Now, in part because of that connection, I'm flying to Mali in December. I'll be an "observer," presumably expert on environmental issues, for the first-ever international conference of a group called OSEDA, the Organization for Social and Environmental Development in Africa. It's concerned in part with connections with the land.

My next-door neighbors here in Debrecen, Istvan and Magdi —a connection I couldn't do without!—introduced me recently to a geologist friend of theirs. Geologists study the land. (Okay, so I'm stretching it a bit—stay with me.) It turns out he's also a Unitarian; I was briefly a Unitarian minister. Now I hope to use that connection to learn more about Unitarianism here.

In my interview with Zoltan Siklosi in an earlier *Bridge*, I said the land here reminds me of Oklahoma. Maybe that's part of why I feel comfortable here, almost at home. My wife, Carole, who is part Cherokee Indian—Native Americans *really* knew about connections with the land!—is already getting her hands into the Hungarian soil. (She's also joining me as a co-expert in Mali!)

The other connections just have to do with people. Just coincidences, I suppose, but they're neat—to use a careful, scholarly word. Just a few examples.

We have two friends in America whose roots are Hungarian, but who have never visited here; we hope they will use our time here as the opportunity to connect with their roots. (One is the niece of the famous Hungarian-American scientist, Leo Szilard, and still remembers some Hungarian from her childhood home in New York.)

In Vienna on fall break, Carole and I just happened to stay at a pension called the Hargita. The family of the woman who owned it came from that region of Transylvania. All the staff spoke Hungarian. One woman who worked there clearly didn't speak English. I was able to impress—and surprise!—her with the few words of Hungarian I have learned.

In the newspaper in our hometown of Ada, Oklahoma, last spring, a good friend of mine noticed a young man named Csaba Kohegyi listed among the graduates from nearby Calvin High School. Realizing, perceptively, that was not a common Okie name, he told us about it, and we took the initiative and met him. He's from Pecs. He visited us here in "the Calvinist Rome" last week.

The last connection has to do with music. And gets the land back into the picture. Sort of. I'm teaching a course on Rock Music and American Culture. In a taxi in Budapest with a driver who spoke very little English, when The Guess Who came on the radio singing "American Woman" (!), he did manage to convey to me that American rock and roll had become a sort of universal language. I love Oklahoma's own great, somewhat radical (but that just has to do with getting back to roots, doesn't it?) folksinger/songwriter, Woody Guthrie. (Bob Dylan is only the best known of the many people he influenced.) During English Week, I'm giving a talk about him, featuring some of his music (on tape). Zoltan will accompany us in a sing-along of Guthrie's famous "This Land is Your Land." (*I* think it ought to be the national anthem!) Sing along: "This land is your land, this land is my land . . ."

We're all connected. To each other. To the Earth.

☮

Just a couple of after-thoughts. We did not get to go to Mali; as I recall, someone embezzled some of the money that was to fund the conference! Notice that when I was given the opportunity to lecture about something I cared about, I chose

Oklahoma's own Woody Guthrie. And I was amazed that Zoltan already knew the melody and some of the lyrics to "This Land." Singing it together with Carole and I the only two Okies present felt really good.

The Bridge rather often featured pieces by or about visiting scholars. Carole and I enjoy playing games, including Trivial Pursuit, so I even wrote one column about that! And another about my all-time favorite musician, Doug Sahm (of The Sir Douglas Quintet, The Texas Tornados, etc.). One issue featured a piece called "The Cherokee Connection," by a student named Linda Vasarhelyi, that featured a picture of Carole and some information about her personal Cherokee connection—Carole is indeed part Cherokee, and as a child even had the Cherokee nickname Erheluha, or Dancing Butterfly. More broadly, I'd say there was a high level of interest in Hungary in all things Native American; Carole said, for example, that bringing that subject up was the way she succeeded in getting her students to start talking!

I need to return to more "scholarly" concerns. Tamas Vrauko and I presented a paper together on "The Reception of American Pop Culture in Hungary Since 1960" at the 1996 European Association for American Studies Biennial Conference at the University of Warsaw, Poland. For my comments, I drew primarily on my experience teaching Rock Music and American Culture at Kossuth. And one of the things I am proudest of in a scholarly sense as I look back on that two years in Hungary is a textbook Tibor Glant and I wrote together, *United States History: A Brief Introduction for Hungarian Students.* Just over 150 pages, it is indeed brief, and it emphasizes political, economic, and diplomatic basics of the American past, while acknowledging the importance of the "new social history," feeling as we did that Hungarian students needed that basic over-view. Indeed, one of the reasons we wrote the book is stated in the Preface: "Teaching American history in Hungary, one quickly becomes aware that one of the persistent problems is the availability of resources, including textbooks." Noting that those that do exist tend to be both too extensive and too expensive for Hungarian students, "We decided to solve that problem by writing our own brief overview of United States history with Hungarian students specifically in mind." When it was possible to bring something into the narrative Hungarian students might be familiar with, we were careful to do so. For example, we note that "many individuals from other countries were moved by the ideals of the American Revolution to volunteer in support of the cause— including Hungarian Colonel Michael Kovats, who is generally credited with being the founder of the American cavalry." We also note early Hungarian visitors to America such as Sandor Boloni-Farkas and Agoston Haraszthy along with the more famous Frenchman Alexis de Tocqueville, all of whom began to comment on the growth of American nationalism and the emergence of a distinctive American "type," and of course the 1851 visit to the U. S. of Louis Kossuth, Hungarian national hero who was hailed here as a democratic hero as well. Our book has gone through three printings, and is used at other universities in addition to Kossuth; it has also been transferred to CD-ROM, along with additional helpful information such as biographical sketches, portraits, documents, statistics, and a glossary. I like to think that Tibor and I made a contribution that continues to help large numbers of Hungarian students to learn American history.

Of course, I also like to claim that I made a contribution by coaching a baseball team while I was in Hungary! Tibor's father lives in Chicago, and he has become a fan of baseball, the Chicago White Sox specifically. One Saturday in Hungary, he called us and asked what we were doing the next morning. We said we had nothing planned, why? His answer: "Let's go to the first-ever baseball game to be played in the city of Debrecen, Hungary." We did. The boys from Debrecen, who called themselves the Dynamites, actually had very little fire-power; they lost 28 to 2! We cheered for them on those rare occasions when they did something good. And we must have been analyzing the game more—and more loudly—than we realized, for when it ended a woman came up to me and said "You seem to know a lot about baseball." I said yes, that I played it when I was younger, loved the game, followed it closely, etc. She said, "These boys need a coach." She was the mother of the first baseman. I agreed to think about it. I met with the team; all of them spoke some English (except the team captain!), and I was impressed. They were a bunch of nice boys, good athletes, but very lacking of the knowledge and skills specifically required for baseball. I checked with my boss at the university, who I'm pretty sure found it a bit weird, but said yes, if I wanted to do it, it was okay. So in addition to being Soros Professor of American Studies at Kossuth University, I became the coach of the Debrecen Dynamites! It was great fun, and served to remind me of my love of the game at a time when a strike by Major League Baseball had given me a sour taste. We achieved some success also, for example losing only 9-8 the next time around to that team that beat us 28-2. The Debrecen Dynamites still exist. And my absolute favorite souvenir of our time in Hungary is a miniature baseball bat, made by my first baseman Akos in his grandfather's woodworking shop, that says "Debrecen Dynamites," and is autographed by each boy along with his uniform number. I'm looking at it as I write this—along with my cap that reads "Coach—Debrecen Dynamites."

I should try to be just a bit more serious about this Hungarian baseball adventure, to make it reflect a little more than just my love of the game: I reviewed the book, *Baseball in Blue & Gray: The National Pastime During the Civil War*, by George Kirsch, for the Fall, 2006, issue of the *Hungarian Journal of English and American Studies*. I began by noting, "Anyone who found it strange that a Soros Professor American Studies would coach a baseball team probably needs to read this book." Seriously, I noted that baseball holds a unique position in American history/ culture, that it was being referred to as the "national game" even before the Civil War, that it has sparked more fine writing than any other sport, that it has so worked its way into popular American slang that even non-baseball fans use such phrases as hitting a home run, striking out, getting to first base. My final paragraph: "Kirsch's final sentence reads, 'The ties between baseball and the American nation first forged in the Civil War continue into the twenty-first century.' Indeed! So it seems perfectly appropriate that a professor of 'American Studies' should coach a baseball team while in Hungary; maybe it should be made a part of the job description?"

I was given an opportunity to say goodbye in *The Bridge* as the end of my stay in Hungary approached. I headed it "Viszontlatasra," which means so long, or see you later. "Earlier this month, in Sulphur Springs, Texas, USA," I noted, "my wife, Carole, and I stood in a circle with my brother, Danny, and my sister-in-law, Claudine, in their living room, toasted 'Egeszsegedre!', and each downed a shot of Unicum." (Egeszsegedre means to your health, or here's to you; Unicum is a liqueur that bills itself as "Hungary's National Drink.") "That may seem a trivial incident," I continued, "but for me it symbolizes the fact that my 'Hungarian adventure' has had an impact on me, in some ways that I am aware of and doubtless in others that I am not aware of yet." I referred to my time there as "a wonderful, broadening, probably life-changing experience." That was May 15, 1996; as I write this, it's May 26, 2010, and I think I was right. After our return, the *ECU Journal* ran a brief piece, including a picture of us standing on a dock by a boat on which we cruised the Danube River and me saying that I was grateful for the opportunity to teach in Hungary and hoped my experience would benefit my students at ECU. I think/hope it did.

Certainly I know that my experiences teaching American history abroad, in both England and Hungary, were incredibly exciting and valuable experiences for me. At the end of my English experience, I contended that the exchange program with Keele was "good for everybody concerned. It's good for their students and faculty and also for TU students and faculty as well as the individual professors involved." I'd say the same for Kossuth and ECU. I began this chapter by suggesting that one doesn't really learn how to teach American history until he or she tries to teach it to non-Americans. I sincerely believe I was a better teacher of American history after my English and Hungarian experiences. I remember for some years using a supplementary book in my American history courses here in the US entitled *As Others See Us*. It consisted of excerpts from textbooks in other countries about topics in US history, for example, a Mexican textbook on our war against Mexico in 1848 and a Russian textbook about the Cold War. Obviously, I felt it would be helpful for my students to see our history from different perspectives. For me, teaching American history abroad was an even more effective way to accomplish that broadening.

CHAPTER 6

Reflections on Using the Same Notes
Throughout a Career

In 2002, I won the Teaching Excellence Award at East
Central University. It was my second time, the first being ten
years earlier. It was also the year I retired, so it felt rather good to
think maybe I still "had it" as I segued into (semi-)retirement.
One of the things we were asked to do after we were nominated
for the award was to write an essay of no more than two pages
called "My Teaching Philosophy." I think it's appropriate here to
share part of what I wrote:

> A few years ago, I was in a stall in a restroom on the second floor
> of the Horace Mann Building, and two of my students,
> obviously not knowing I could hear them, were talking about my
> class, United States History Survey to 1877. One said to the
> other, "Man, that Dr. Joyce is really intense, isn't he?" The other
> responded, "Yeah, I don't understand why he's so passionate
> about that stuff."
>
> Quite frankly, I believe that if I have any claim to "Teaching
> Excellence," it is that I am "so passionate about that stuff" that I
> teach. I love history. I love teaching. I love students, working with
> them, struggling at times to even get them to pay attention, and
> once in a great while, just often enough to keep me going, seeing
> that light come on in their eyes that shows that I do indeed have
> their attention, that I'm getting through, that they are actually
> listening and thinking.
>
> I think being knowledgeable and well organized are the next two
> most important things after passion. And I feel pretty
> comfortable with myself in both those areas, continue to work
> hard at them, even as I approach retirement. But I would
> emphasize most the passion. Isn't part of why we are called

"professors" that we have something to profess, something that we care deeply about and wish to impart to others?

You see, while I sometimes get frustrated with our students (their lack of maturity, motivation, and study skills), as I know many of my colleagues do, I also identify with them a great deal. I'm from a small town in this part of the country myself (Greenwood, Arkansas), and I remember feeling very unprepared for and overwhelmed by the initial experience of college. Some sensitive professors helped me make it. I hope to play that role for our students, many of whom remind me of myself at that stage.

But I also believe that part of our job in higher education is to grab students who come to us and shake them out of their lethargy, to challenge the comfortable little cliches to which they've been exposed, to broaden their world view and show them alternative ways of seeing things. I find historiography, an approach which emphasizes different interpretations of important historical subjects, one way to do that. I've been know to say to students something like, "You'll probably forget, and soon, that Grover Cleveland was the first Democrat elected to the presidency after the Civil War. And that's okay. But I hope you won't forget how to think critically, to evaluate what you read, what you hear, including from me, and most of all how to see the impact of history continuing in the events of your own life."

Seeing the impact of history in their own lives—that's one of the central objectives in the way I teach history. I even state that on my syllabus in the survey course. It's not an opinion or an interpretation, I tell them, that history has an impact on their life. It does, indisputably. We each individually, and collectively as a people, walk around with the burden and glory of our history every day. The only question is whether we're attuned to that, smart enough to pay attention to that, to learn from that. History is relevant, I tell them—to draw on a popular word from the 60s when I completed my training as a historian and began to try to be one—not in the sense that it is going to save the world; no academic discipline is going to do that. But relevant in the sense that approached properly (with an open, inquiring mind, a willingness to read, to think, to question everything, including perhaps most of all the things you think you absolutely know), history can help to provide us a storehouse of information on the basis of which we can make more intelligent decisions about our lives, our country, our world.

It's easy, I noted, for most individuals to see the importance of their background (their family, community, church, school, etc.) in making them who they are, and helping them decide what they want to be, but harder to do that collectively, as a country, a people. "But that's the challenge to which I try to rise every semester, to try to get my students to rise."

I quoted with pride some student comments on evaluation forms: "He is very well informed on a variety of subjects—promotes stimulating conversation and challenges us to think." "Dr. Joyce is very passionate about what he is teaching. He gets the class fired up, wanting to know more . . . ." "I have never seen anyone so excited over his subject matter . . . ." And finally, on a different but I think equally important note: "He helps students by providing study sessions before the tests and his office is always open to students."

And finally, here's how I concluded my teaching philosophy statement:

> Just two more points relevant to my teaching philosophy. I take some pride in the research and writing that I have done. But I take the most pride in the fact that my research and writing have never taken away from my teaching, indeed that I have always been able to relate the two. Most of my research and publication activity has been in the area of American historiography, so it's been fairly easy to relate that to my teaching. (I'm assuming here that at least some readers of this statement will have experienced the phenomenon of having a professor so involved in research and publication that he/she is unable/unwilling to devote time to students and to teaching.) At a regional state university like East Central, teaching is what we do; nothing should be allowed to divert us from that as our central activity, and from doing it the best we possibly can.

> Finally, I began by saying something about what I perceive to be my reputation among students. In addition to being known as passionate, I think I am known as tough. Tough in terms of academic standards, tough in terms of tolerating nothing less than mature behavior in the classroom. I don't cringe at that reputation; rather, I treasure it. But even more importantly, I hope and believe that it is known that there's not a professor here who will do more to help students do well if they are willing to do the work. Some of our students—sad to say, an increasingly large percentage, it seems—come to us without the aforementioned maturity, motivation, and study skills. And that's not really their fault, is it? A big part of our job is to take them where they are and help them develop. We do that, I think, in part, by placing the bar high for both personal behavior and academic performance. But we are also obligated as professors, as professionals, to give everything we have to help them do their best. What a challenge! What an exciting, important challenge!

Eight years later as I write this, I still feel that way! I guess it's part of why I haven't been able to give up teaching entirely, but plan to return to teach one more course this fall at Rogers State University.

Why, you might ask, would a person who feels that way about teaching use the same lecture notes throughout a career?! Carrying it a step further, Carole asked why I would want to write a chapter *called* that. It's true that I used until the day I retired in 2002 the same hand-written notes that I worked up as a graduate student pursuing my Ph.D. in history at the University of Oklahoma in the academic year 1964-1965. But by no means does that suggest that I was stuck in a rut; rather, my methods and interpretations changed dramatically over the years. The original set of notes smells a bit like mildew from being stored foolishly under our house here in Spavinaw for a while, and they're quite yellowed, but otherwise still in pretty good shape. And yes, in case you're wondering, I even took them to England and Hungary.

Part of understanding how I could use the same notes and yet evolve so differently lies in my commitment to historiography. David M. Wrobel wrote a thoughtful article about this in the Spring, 2008, issue of the excellent little pedagogical journal *Teaching History: A Journal of Methods*. He called it "Historiography as Pedagogy: Thoughts About the Messy Past and Why We Shouldn't Clean It Up." "Historiography is vital to our teaching about the past and to our understanding of the present," he begins, "though you would not always know as much from the practices of K-16 history educators." He tells of a "well-meaning colleague" who advised him early in his career to "Avoid historiography like the plague" because "students just did not care about the changing views and perspectives of historians over time." Instead, he says, he wound up "making it the foundation" of his teaching over the years. He insists, convincingly I think, that "If you want students to understand the dynamism and the relevance of the past, then you have to let them know that the past is and always has been the subject of debate, not just for politicians and historians, but for all people who want to understand their world." Finally: "I try to illuminate contemporary issues by emphasizing how scholars have viewed historical trends and events differently at different moments in time. This is historiography—the history of historical writing and thinking. Or, to offer a more vital explanation: Historiography is the study of the dynamic past, a past that is always messy, ever changing, never resolved, and always relevant to the present."

But why would a person who became that committed to historiography continue to use those notes? I guess, for some time, I needed them as an outline of events; even later, I "needed" them for security. I remember my mentor at the University of Oklahoma in those days, John S. Ezell, responding to someone's question in the graduate assistant group that was starting to teach at the university level for the first time, "When will we ever get over these butterflies in the stomach?" Dr. Ezell's answer, basically, was: "Never. If you do, you're not taking it seriously enough, and it's time to do something else."

I haven't really explained that the notes I'm referring to are for History 3 and 4 at OU, the United States History Survey to and since 1865. The textbook in use in those days was John D. Hicks, *The Federal Union*, 4th edition. (That was the volume that came up to the Civil War; the volume that came from the war to the present was called *The American Nation*.) As I recall, I also read and used extensively in putting my lecture notes together *A Synopsis of American History*, by Charles Sellers and Henry May. I figured I not only needed to stay a few pages ahead of my students in the textbook, but use an additional source or two as well!

I still think those old notes are good in terms of providing a basic overview of American history. But I look at some parts of them and see fundamental differences in them and what I was teaching by the end of my career. I see, for example, in my notes, that when I was dealing with Andrew Jackson and Jacksonian Democracy, I talked about Jackson's election as the so-called "Revolution of 1828," I emphasized the "common man" coming of age in American politics; that Jackson was a man of minimal political experience and education, essentially just a military hero; the concept (or at least the practice) of a strong presidency, using his veto power more than the six previous presidents altogether and seeing his cabinet members as essentially "errand boys" and relying more on his inner circle sometimes called the "kitchen cabinet;" his use of the spoils system and even rotation in office; and, finally, the introduction of a truly national political party machine. That's all true, basically, but by the end of my career, though it doesn't say so in those notes, I would never have lectured about Jackson without saying he was racist, sexist, violent, anti-intellectual. Racist? He thought if you were Black he ought to own you, and if you were Native American he ought to kill you—or at the very least drive you from your homeland. Sexist? Yes, he put women on a pedestal, and if you have a romantic bone in your body you should be moved by the story of his relationship with his wife Rachel, but that definitely does *not* mean he regarded women as equals of men. Violent? The evidence suggests that if Andrew Jackson got angry at you, he thought he ought to beat you up, or shoot you, and if his country got angry at your country, the thing to do was go to war. Anti-intellectual? Let me be sure to make a distinction here: I am *not* putting Jackson down for being uneducated; I *am* putting him down for apparently distrusting people who *were* educated, who were intellectuals. (Richard Hofstadter helped me understand many years ago, in his book, *Anti-Intellectualism in American Life,* just what a powerful strand that has been in America.) So with this as one example, it might be suggested that my original notes were a starting point for my coverage, but that my coverage expanded and evolved over the years.

I remember vividly the first lecture I ever gave in a university classroom. I was assigned to work for Donald J. Berthrong as a graduate assistant. He insisted I should lecture once, that it would help prepare me for teaching, which I was scheduled to do the next semester. (I first taught, as I've mentioned, in the fall of 1964, so this was probably in the spring semester of that year.) This was a large survey course in US history since the Civil War, probably 150 students or so. My topic was the 1920s. I had a good set of notes worked up, I thought. (Of course, I still have them.) But I was a nervous wreck. The class was supposed to be an hour and fifteen minutes in length, but without realizing it, I plowed through *all* the notes I had in about forty-five minutes! I asked if there were any questions. I think I had gone so fast, covered so much, that they were overwhelmed, couldn't think of anything to ask. So I said "Class dismissed." Dr. Berthrong came walking up the aisle with a gentle, knowing smile on his face, and said, basically, "You had some good material, but you need to slow down a little bit."

That story suggests that not only did I change in terms of interpretation over the years, but also in terms of the amount of detail covered. I had so much detail in my lecture notes by the time I got done with them that they were better for use in upper-level period courses I taught (Colonial America, Early National Era, Jacksonian America) than in surveys.

But one more story about interpretation. My Ph.D. dissertation, written under the supervision of Dr. Ezell, was a study of the life and writings of historian Edward Channing. With some revision (not much, since Dr. Ezell was such a taskmaster!), it became my first book in 1974. But I wrote a book in 1983 which is my least favorite of all my books. It's called *History and Historians: Some Essays*. One of those essays was "Edward Channing and the Negro," originally presented as a paper at the 1979 meeting of the Southern Historical Association. I noted in the brief introduction to the essay that I wrote for the book that the critic assigned to the SHA session dealt rather severely with my paper, insisting that I had not been hard enough on Channing for being a racist. Then I wrote:

> I feel that I made it amply clear that Channing was a racist, and that that racism, for today, must be condemned. But moral indignation, while appealing at an emotional level, contributes little to the historian's craft; the soap-box is seldom an appropriate place for the historian. Besides, what does it accomplish to point the accusatory finger at a historical figure— or in this case a historian? I have left the paper unchanged.

I shared that passage with my good friend and colleague at East Central University, Scott Barton, sometime in the 1990s, and he said, "Davis, that's awful; I can't believe you ever wrote anything like that!" I can't believe I did either! But I did. I was still in a defensive mode in part, I suppose, defending myself against the critic, who had indeed been quite harsh. But hopefully, if you've read to this point, you know that I came to feel very strongly that moral indignation contributes a great deal to the historian's craft, indeed that it is essential. What other stance is appropriate when confronted with racism, sexism, war, injustice? I had begun to read the works of Howard Zinn, certainly, by the time I wrote and presented that paper at the SHA in 1979, but clearly I had not allowed his approach to influence me adequately! While it's embarrassing to share that story, and especially that quote, I do so to emphasize my change over time, and the need for all of us to change over time, and the assistance historiography can provide in that process.

Back, specifically, to my lecture notes. Allow me to stroll through them, specifically the first half of the survey course, since it was more my specialty—I think I can make some interesting points.

Occasionally, I'm just reminded that we, historians, learned more over time. In my notes, I suggest that the native population of the area now the United States before European arrival might have been one million. I'm pretty sure most experts now say it was likely ten times that, some even more. Though my notes still just show the earlier figure, I remember that I did indeed tell students that the figure was gradually being revised upward over the years. It makes a difference, doesn't it? One million . . .not that many. Ten million . . . hmmm.

Occasionally also, my mostly-factual notes show a distinct point of view—and sometimes it's even one that I'm still comfortable with, like my insistence that the Puritans, while they came to America for toleration, became quite intolerant themselves, including their expulsion of Roger Williams from the colony of Massachusetts for two "heretical" beliefs that I obviously agreed with him on: complete separation of church and state, and his insistence that "Indians" had certain rights the white man should respect.

I clearly enjoyed, even as a graduate teaching assistant in 1964, bursting popular bubbles. After talking about all the significant foreign assistance the colonies had in the American Revolutionary War, I said the idea that "thirteen little colonies whipped the great nation of Great Britain" was a farce—"It was more like 'the colonies *and Europe* versus the little island of Great

Britain!" And following up on Shays' Rebellion, and the Washington administration's overwhelming response, I said, "Southerners remember: Washington, a Southern conservative, first used forceful federal intervention in a state!" In a similar vein, I find a note that I apparently inserted later. After dealing with the mention of secession as a possibility by some New England states at the Hartford Convention at the end of the War of 1812, I have this quote from an editorial in *The Richmond Observer:* "No man, no association of men, no state or set of states has a right to withdraw itself from this Union of its own accord . . . any attempt to dissolve the Union or to obstruct the efficacy of its constitutional laws is Treason—Treason to all intents and purposes." I followed that quote with the simple note "contrast with 1860." But I'm pretty sure I remember raving a bit about how the people of Richmond, and even more the political leaders of the so-called "Confederacy" that considered Richmond its capitol, should have read that editorial.

Sometimes I showed an interest in "social history," which was not yet the big deal it became, and sometimes I later added in the margin of my notes the names of historians. One example: I had a brief section following the basic factual outline of the American Revolution on "The American Revolution as a social revolution," a section which emphasized things like "all men created equal," upper class types (Tories) fleeing the colonies in significant numbers, early movements in the northern colonies especially to abolish slavery, efforts to abolish other "artificial" inequalities such as primogeniture and entail, the first slight break in the overwhelmingly agricultural nature of the country and the beginning of manufacturing, and the fact that some state constitutions sometimes included wider suffrage provisions and bills of rights. In the margin, obviously added later, was "Jameson," by which I clearly meant *The American Revolution Considered as a Social Movement,* by J. Franklin Jameson.

Embarrassment is not so common when I look at the old notes, but once in a while, that's the only way to respond. In listing reasons for westward expansion, I actually had "lull in the Indian menace." Menace?! I actually said "there were two sides even to slavery." Really?! Fortunately, I know for sure that early on I began to revise my presentation in both those cases. And again, at times I was already blunt in a way consistent with my later viewpoints, as in "Mexican War largely an imperialistic war on our part—we wanted the territory, and started war to get it."

Finally, I was never much interested in military history. In the notes as I first worked them up, I devoted about 1/3 of a page in my Civil War section to "the war itself." I can't remember if I had complaints about that, or what, but I do see that I early on added material that extended that topic to four full pages!

For the second half survey course, from the Civil War to the present, the notes do not actually come up to the present. Rather, the detailed notes stop essentially with the end of World War II —after that, there's just about a page and a half which lists possible topics to talk about in the post-war era. Bear in mind that I first taught the course in 1965, so the list of topics is headed "1945-1965, both foreign and domestic, strictly chronological and strictly *major* things—informal, with hopefully lots of discussion." I also see that I added topics over the years, including Presidential elections. But what I remember even more is that early on I began to realize that taking an autobiographical approach to the history I lived through would be best, especially for making my point about how history has an impact on our lives. I can't imagine how many times I told students about being born in western Arkansas in the summer of 1940 (and how my Mom always talked about the incredible heat and humidity—no electricity—more than the pain of childbirth) just a short time before the government came in and bought out all the families in the area to create Fort Chaffee. Foreign affairs, I noted, including the events leading to World War II, had a profound impact on my life when I was just a baby. I told stories about my experience with race, including, of course, the one about me and my friend Robert in Shamrock, Texas. And I used this autobiographical approach to try to get students thinking about the impact of history on *their* lives for the first time. Sometimes it worked. I can remember, at East Central University, suggesting that students talk with their parents, or more likely grandparents, about the Great Depression/Dust Bowl era, and having some of them come back to class with incredibly powerful stories. "I thought history was just a bunch of dates and stuff you memorized out of a textbook," said one. This approach also emphasizes "people's history," as made famous by Howard Zinn and others, that is to say, *all* of us, We the People, are part of history.

So, did I keep the same notes I originally worked up at the University of Oklahoma in 1964-1965 and use them to a certain extent throughout my career? Yes. But I evolved, I like to think in positive ways. I was not as tied to my notes, I became increasingly receptive to new interpretations, I was more inclusive. I learned that statistics about unemployment in the Great Depression, which were included in my notes, might not be as effective as telling how my Dad had a job at a little rural grocery store in western Arkansas through those years making $1.25 a day, and told us many times that he thanked God every day he had that job, because so many people he knew didn't have work at all. I learned that it probably didn't work as well for me to lecture, even to rant and rave, about how World War I was yet another rich man's war/poor man's fight, as it did to have a student speak up who had interviewed his grandfather and learned that he had been a participant in the Green Corn Rebellion, an inter-racial uprising against World War I partially located in Pontotoc County where East Central itself was located.

I learned, in short, that it's not a bad thing to keep the same lecture notes throughout your career—as long as you're not tied to them.

CHAPTER 7

The Wisdom (and Wit) of Will (and Ariel) Durant
Possible Lessons for Teachers and Students

This piece originally appeared in the Spring, 2005, issue of the *East Central University Research Journal*, which was then edited by my friend Alvin O. Turner, a fellow historian who is now retired as Dean of the School of Humanities and Social Sciences at East Central. Al noted in his introductory comments for the issue that it "marks a significant shift in its [the journal's] content and purposes with increased attention to ECU student research and writing . . . ." And he said this of my essay specifically: "Joyce's paper on the wit and wisdom found in Will and Ariel Durant's *Story of Civilization* seemed especially appropriate for this issue because of its concern with teaching and the link between that endeavor and student learning." Hopefully the reader will consider it "especially appropriate" for inclusion here as well. Note that my "personal" connection—in the "personal/ historical" phrase—is certainly not the same here as in other parts of this work, since the Durants' final volume in the series carries the story only through *The Age of Napoleon*, yet over the years of reading the Durants' historical work, I did indeed come to feel a strong connection to it personally. The Durants' work is interdisciplinary in nature, which I like, and many of the same themes appear there that appear elsewhere in this book, including religion, race, class, war and peace, the relevance of history.

☮

At both universities where I spent most of my career, the University of Tulsa and East Central University, I had at least one colleague who found it incomprehensible that I read Will Durant's *The Story of Civilization*. This criticism was never subtle. I remember being told that I was wasting my time, asked how a professional historian could possibly read that stuff, reminded that Durant was a philosopher rather than a historian and such a generalist that any specialist would find him wrong in his/her field—I even remember being laughed at. But I persevered. I read the entire eleven volumes. Twice. And enjoyed it. And learned a lot doing it. Fortunately, at East Central University, I had one colleague who could rise above narrow professional/specialist attitudes and share my love of Durant. He could see that there was much of value in *The Story of Civilization*, including both wit and wisdom; he had read portions of it many years before, and frequently amazed me by remembering a segment as if he had just read it the day before, so that we could have long conversations about it. This article is dedicated to the memory of that colleague, Lloyd Wayne Goss.

Part of what I believe is that Durant's series is indeed full of wisdom. And wit. Indeed, Durant reminds us that the two words, wit and wisdom, have a common origin and close relationship to each other—and to the word *veda* from India, which means knowledge. In *Heroes of History: A Brief History of Civilization from Ancient Times to the Dawn of the Modern Age*, a volume actually completed by others and published in 2001, twenty years after Durant's death, he quoted Solon: "I grow old, while always learning."[1] Durant's *Story of Civilization* series can help with that learning process. Shall we work our way through each of the eleven volumes looking for some examples? Even if you are not inspired to overcome any professional snobbery of which you may be guilty—all of us are, to some degree, in some ways—and actually read Durant, perhaps you can learn something. And perhaps you can share it with your students—whether in history, philosophy, religion, sociology, political science, geography, art, education, even mathematics and the sciences.

The first volume, *Our Oriental Heritage*, was published in 1935. It was dedicated to Durant's wife, Ariel; her role in the series became so important that her name was added as coauthor beginning with the seventh volume. In the preface, Durant acknowledged the difficulty of a single person telling the entire story of civilization. "I do not need to be told how absurd this enterprise is," he wrote, "nor how immodest is its very conception . . . ." Still, he had "dreamed that despite the many errors inevitable in this undertaking, it may be of some use to those upon whom the passion for philosophy has laid the compulsion to try to see things whole . . . ." He was aware the specialists would give him a hard time—"any man who sells his soul to synthesis will be a tragic target for a myriad merry darts of specialist critique." Indeed; even in 1935, and more so later. But Durant made the case strongly that "our usual method of writing history in separate longitudinal sections"—economic, political, and religious history, the history of philosophy, literature, science, music, art—"does injustice to the unity of human life . . . ." Is there not wisdom even in these opening claims? "I shall proceed as rapidly as time and circumstance will permit," he wrote, acknowledging the difficulty of his undertaking and the potential for it taking a very long time indeed if he could complete it at all, "hoping that a few of my contemporaries will care to grow old with me while learning [a la Solon], and that these volumes may help some of our children to understand and enjoy the infinite riches of their inheritance."[2]

Durant begins by defining civilization; it is, he suggests, "social order promoting cultural creation," and four elements constitute it: "economic provision, political organization, moral traditions, and the pursuit of knowledge and the arts." Certain factors condition it, and may encourage it or impede it, primarily geological, geographic, and economic conditions. Ahead of his time, perhaps anticipating Jared Diamond's 1996 Pulitzer Prize-winning work *Guns, Germs, and Steel: The Fates of Human Societies*,[3] Durant insisted that "There are no racial conditions to civilization. It may appear on any continent and in any color . . . ."[4]

"Let us, before we die, gather up our heritage, and offer it to our children,"[5] concludes Durant's preface, again mindful of the importance of passing our civilization and knowledge of it on to our children. Indeed, let us do so.

In this first volume—devoted to the Near East (Sumeria, Egypt, Babylonia, Assyria, Judea, and Persia), India, and the Far East (China and Japan)—Durant shows both sensitivity and a prejudice which might be expected of a white male writing in the 1930s. The so-called "savage" is really civilized, he insists, "for he carefully transmits to his children the heritage of the tribe . . . . [I]n calling other human beings 'savage' or 'barbarous' we may be expressing no objective fact, but only our fierce fondness for ourselves, and our timid shyness in the presence of alien ways." The crucial difference between the so-called primitive and the so-called civilized, he suggests, is literacy.[6]   And perhaps that definition helps to explain the afore-mentioned prejudice, that is, the virtual exclusion of the peoples of most of Africa and all of America from "the story of civilization." But Durant is able to see good even in societies from those lands. Quoting explorer Robert Edwin Peary's story about asking one of his Eskimo guides "Of what are you thinking?" and the guide responding "I do not have to think; I have plenty of meat," Durant concluded, "Not to think unless we have to—there is much to be said for this as the summation of wisdom."[7]

Can today's students handle the kind of insights Durant so often provides, for example, in such areas as religion and gender relations? One hopes so. He refers to "the almost universal myth of a god dying for his people, and then returning triumphantly to life." And he concludes that "a certain tension between religion and society marks the higher stages of every civilization." Elaborating: "Religion begins by offering magical aid to harassed and bewildered men; it culminates by giving to people that unity of morals and belief which seems so favorable to statesmanship and art; it ends by fighting suicidally in the lost cause of the past." On gender: "For the most part primitive women asked of clothing precisely what later women have asked—not that it should quite cover their nakedness, but that it should enhance or suggest their charms. Everything changes, except woman and man."[8]

In a chapter entitled "The Prehistoric Beginnings of Civilization," the final one of introductory material before beginning his treatment of the Oriental cultures, Durant suggests that "In one sense all human history hinges upon two revolutions: the neolithic passage from hunting to agriculture, and the modern passage from agriculture to industry; no other revolutions have been quite as real or basic as these."[9] Is that still valid in 2005, in terms of the computer revolution, for example? It's certainly worth a discussion.

The first specific Near Eastern culture with which he deals, Sumeria, impressed Durant. It was a culture which indicated "a refinement of life and manners disturbing to our naive conception of progress as a continuous rise of man through the unfortunate cultures of the past to the unrivaled zenith of today."[10]

Moving on to the Egyptians, Durant's take is interesting, and in at least one case perhaps an unexpected one. Writing of the Pyramids, surely the most famous symbol of that civilization, he insists that "there is something barbarically primitive—or barbarically modern—in this brute hunger for size." All things considered, it is really only "the memory and imagination of the beholder that, swollen with history, make these monuments great," for "in themselves they are a little ridiculous—vainglorious tombs in which the dead sought eternal life." Durant even thinks photography has "too much ennobled them," for it "can catch everything but dirt, and enhances man-made objects with noble vistas of land and sky." His conclusion: "The sunset at Gizeh is greater than the Pyramids."[11]

On other aspects of Egyptian civilization, Durant is equally thoughtful. Noting the diverse ethnic make-up of the Egyptian people, he insisted that "even at that date there were no pure races on the earth." Discussing Egyptian military activities, specifically the subjugation of Syria, he observed that Thutmose I "returned to Thebes laden with spoils and the glory that always comes from the killing of men." Cynical? Certainly a valid historical observation. A reference to one ruler who "built a wall twenty-seven miles long" earned a footnote: "This word [built], when used in reference to rulers, must always be understood as a euphemism." Some things never change. Impressed by Egypt's educational accomplishments—"not till the nineteenth century of our era was the public instruction of the young to be so well organized again"—Durant also admits that "the chief problem, as ever, was discipline," and quotes one teacher lamenting that his pupils "love books much less than beer." Egypt, says Durant, was "a land which, like all others, looked upon itself as the only civilized country in the world." History itself had already advanced (?) to its modern style: "Official historians accompanied the Pharaohs on their expeditions, never saw their defeats, and recorded, or invented, the details of their victories; already the writing of history had become a cosmetic art."[12]

Durant's treatment of Babylonia is briefer. "Never was a civilization richer in superstitions," he suggests. After listing some of them—including the belief that the fate of a king could be forecast by observing the movements of a dog—he concluded that they seem ridiculous to us only because they differ ("superficially") from our own (example: foretelling the length of winter "by spying upon the groundhog"). "There is hardly an absurdity of the past that cannot be found flourishing somewhere in the present. Underneath all civilization, ancient or modern, moved and still moves a sea of magic, superstition and sorcery. Perhaps they will remain when the works of our reason have passed away."[13]

Durant's coverage of Persia is not as extensive as one might expect, but perhaps deserves treatment here in part because of its relevance today. Quoting first the Zoroastrian religion's version of the Golden Rule—"That nature alone is good which shall not do unto another whatever is not good unto its own self"—he then notes another of their scriptures—"Wicked is he who is good to the wicked"—and cleverly concludes: "Inspired works are seldom consistent." Durant frequently emphasized unchanging human nature, the universality of history. Having described Xerxes I as "every inch a king," which meant among other things that he was both handsome and vain, Durant concluded that "there was never yet a handsome man who was not vain, nor any physically

vain man whom some woman has not led by the nose." Sexist?
Perhaps, but as usual with Durant, surely worthy of—and
stimulating of—a discussion. "[A]n empire exists only so long as
it retains its superior capacity to kill," insists Durant unarguably.
And: "It is in the nature of an empire to disintegrate soon, for
the energy that created it disappears from those who inherit it, at
the very time that its subject peoples are gathering strength to
fight for their lost liberty."[14]

India, China, and Japan are each treated extensively, of
course, but we must settle for just an example or so from each of
Durant's wisdom and wit. And noting that historical
understandings of the level of civilization of ancient India had
recently (1930s) changed—"In the days when historians
supposed that history had begun with Greece, Europe gladly
believed that India had been a hotbed of barbarism until the
'Aryan' cousins of the European peoples had migrated from the
shores of the Caspian to bring the arts and sciences to a savage
and benighted peninsula"—he showed both wit and wisdom in
his knowledge that just as recent research had "marred this
comforting picture," so "future researches will change the
perspective of these pages."[15] Seldom are historians so willing
and able to admit that their views will prove transient. But of
course they will.

Quoting Yajnavalkya's suggestion that the ideal state
(heaven?) would be for the individual to have no individual
consciousness—"As flowing rivers disappear in the sea, losing
their name and form, thus a wise man, freed from name and
form, goes to the divine person who is beyond all"—Durant then
notes that "Such a theory of life and death will not please
Western man, whose religion is as permeated with individualism
as are his political and economic institutions." Yet he seems
almost hopeful when he speculates, "Perhaps, in return for
conquest, arrogance and spoliation, India will teach us the
tolerance and gentleness of the mature mind, the quiet content
of the unacquisitive soul, the calm of the understanding spirit,
and a unifying, pacifying love for all living things." One "lesson"
Durant draws from India's history is somehow vaguely
disturbing. The "secret" of the political history of modern India,

he suggests, is that weakened by division, it succumbed to invaders who impoverished it; then, losing all power of resistance, it took refuge in purely supernatural consolations and "argued that both mastery and slavery were superficial delusions, and concluded that freedom of the body or the nation was hardly worth defending in so brief a life." Durant's conclusion: "The bitter lesson that may be drawn from this tragedy is that eternal vigilance is the price of civilization. A nation must love peace, but keep its powder dry." Never mind that this seems more simplistic than usual for Durant; one also wonders if he would have seen this issue differently in the atomic age, post-World War II. Suggesting again the possibility of a reversal of fortunes for East and West—the former might go in for science and industry, the latter for a "mystic faith"—Durant concludes: "There is no humorist like history."[16] Of course, it might be noted that few professional historians, or other academics, are so in touch with that aspect of their field and their job as Will Durant.

Frequently, one is simply tempted to take Durant's generalizations and test them in other times and places. Two more examples from his treatment of India must suffice. Religion, he says, "does not prosper under prosperity." And "it is difficult to be at once modest and a reformer."[17]

Showing a deep appreciation of art, in this case in his coverage of China, Durant insists that placing a price on specific pieces of Chinese porcelain is almost "sacrilege," for "the world of beauty and the world of money never touch, even when beautiful things are sold. It is enough to say that Chinese porcelain is the summit and symbol of Chinese civilization, one of the noblest things that men have done to make their species forgivable on the earth."[18]

Sometimes one can only note and lament the timing of history. What Durant wrote about Japan: "The Japanese have studied our civilization carefully, in order to absorb its values and surpass us. Perhaps we should be wise to study their civilization as patiently as they have studied ours, so that when the crisis comes that must issue either in war or understanding, we may be capable of understanding." What happened: Relations between the United States and Japan quickly deteriorated—Durant was writing, remember, in 1935—culminating in events at Pearl Harbor in 1941. Still, surely, the understanding Durant sought is important. As ever, Durant was aware of the possibility of error and the unpredictability of history. "The first lesson of philosophy," he wrote, "is that we may all be mistaken."[19] How true.

Durant recognized the importance of what came before Greece, and the importance of areas other than Greece, but he did insist on the centrality of Greece in understanding (Western) civilization; the entire second volume of *The Story of Civilization* is devoted to *The Life of Greece*. As usual, some of the best, most challenging insights are in Durant's treatment of religion. Taking note of changing Greek gods, he concludes: "The gods are mortal, but piety is everlasting." And noting that in Greek history, "Time and again truces are violated, solemn promises are broken, envoys are slain," he concludes: "Perhaps, however, the Greeks differ from ourselves not in conduct but in candor; our greater delicacy makes it offensive to us to preach what we practice." That remark, obviously, is not confined to religion. But religion certainly is the focus when Durant discusses Euhemerus of Messana's *Hiera Anagrapha* (Holy Scriptures) and its insistence that "gods" were merely personified powers of nature or human heroes deified by popular imagination, then concludes that the book "had a sharply atheistic effect." "Skepticism, however," Durant continues, "is uncomfortable; it leaves the common heart and imagination empty, and the vacuum soon draws in some new and encouraging creed." Finally, religion in relation to philosophy is Durant's subject when he writes that the Greeks "offered the East philosophy, the East offered Greece religion; religion won because philosophy was a luxury for the few, religion was a consolation for the many."[20]

Aristophanes is "an unclassifiable mixture of beauty, wisdom, and filth . . . the most contemporary of ancient poets, for nothing is so timeless as obscenity." Addressing the difficulty sometimes of gleaning clear meaning from philosophers, including Plato—and remember that Durant's major field was philosophy; his 1926 *The Story of Philosophy* was so unexpectedly successful that it allowed him to retire from teaching and devote his energies to *The Story of Civilization*—Durant noted that "Antiphanes said humorously that just as, in a far northern city, words froze into ice as they were spoken, and were heard in the summer when they thawed, so the words spoken by Plato to his students in their youth were finally understood by them only in their old age."[21] Any student (or teacher!) who has struggled for meaning in the work of a philosopher can identify with this. And we can only hope that what we "teach" our students will be "learned" by them later in life.

Aristotle noted three types of government: monarchy (government by power), aristocracy (government by birth), and timocracy (government by excellence). Notice Durant's interesting assertion in the midst of a quote from Aristotle: "'Though one form of government may be better than others,' reads a sentence which every American should memorize, 'yet there is no reason to prevent another from being preferable to it under particular conditions.'"[22] One cannot be sure what Durant had specifically in mind with his inserted comment. But his views clearly contradicted an apparent American belief of the 1970s that if the people of Vietnam democratically chose communism, there was something wrong with democracy. And what about the again-apparent belief of many Americans, including some of our political leaders, that it is no problem to impose American-style democracy at the point of a gun on peoples in various parts of the world?

Sometimes it is tempting to read Durant in such a way as to reenforce one's own heresies, so to speak. (Is the previous paragraph an example?) I have never been much interested in military history; my primary interest in wars is what causes them, the harm they do, how to prevent them. Durant, writing of Ptolemy III: "We shall not follow the record of his wars, for though there is drama in the details of strife, there is a dreary eternity in its causes and results; such history becomes a menial attendance upon the vicissitudes of power, in which victories and defeats cancel one another into a resounding zero." Even better, writing of Archimedes: "The Roman general erected to his memory a handsome tomb, on which was engraved, in accordance with the mathematician's expressed wish, a sphere within a cylinder; to have found formulas for the area and volume of these figures was, in Archimedes' view, the supreme achievement of his life. He was not far wrong; for to add one significant proposition to geometry is of greater value to humanity than to besiege or defend a city."[23]

But enough of Greece. At least here it must be enough. On to Rome, or, as Durant called his third volume, *Caesar and Christ*. "The older Romans used temples as their banks, as we use banks as our temples," he wrote in 1944; sometimes the truth of his assertions makes us squirm. "If we try to reduce to some logical form the passionate disorder of Lucretius' argument, his initial thesis lies in a famous line: *Tantum religio potuit suadere malorum*—'to so many evils religion has persuaded men.'" How often has one human army marched into battle against what they perceive as an "evil" religion while using their own religion to justify their slaughter? Horace warned his readers of the "praiser of times past," insisted that "if some god were for taking you back to those days you would refuse every time," and Durant asserts against the "good old days" phenomenon that "the chief charm of the past is that we know we need not live it again."[24]

It is perhaps fortunate that Durant soon turns to Tacitus, who thought that the "chief duty of the historian is to judge the actions of men, so that the good may meet with the reward due to virtue, and pernicious citizens may be deterred by the condemnation that awaits evil deeds at the tribunal of posterity." Durant insists that this is "a strange conception, which turns history into a Last Judgment and the historian into God." So conceived, Durant continues, "history is a sermon—ethics teaching by horrible examples—and falls, as Tacitus assumed, under the rubric of rhetoric." Finally: "It is easy for indignation to be eloquent but hard for it to be fair; no moralist should write history."[25] Strong stuff. But, is the "objectivity" historians have always presumably sought possible? Is it even desirable? Must not history ultimately address the present and its concerns? For the past, after all, has no concerns. Must not the historian, as human, indeed be a moralist?

Maybe Durant would say that what I am doing here is preaching a sermon. But isn't he preaching also at times? The priestly class known as the Druids, he noted, "to appease the gods . . . offered human sacrifice of men condemned to death for crime;" then he concluded that this custom would "appear barbarous to those who have not seen an electrocution."[26] Why *do* we humans have such a capacity to condemn the atrocities of the past while continuing blind to our own?

Since we're talking about sermons, let's talk about religion, as Durant so often and so insightfully does. Plutarch "almost founded the study of comparative religion by his treatises on Roman and Egyptian cults," thought Durant. "All deities, he argued, are aspects of one supreme being, timeless, indescribable . . . ." Durant speaks in a similar vein, that is to say with apparent admiration, of one Demonax, who, "[i]ndicted before an Athenian court for refusing to offer sacrifice to the gods, . . . won acquittal by saying simply that the gods had no need of offerings, and that religion consisted in kindness to all."[27]

Some would contend that Jesus of Nazareth held that same view of what was essential in religion. Durant's extensive treatment of Jesus and early Christianity is extremely interesting, and perhaps presents at times some of the greatest challenges for students of today who are familiar only with their own particular approach to Christianity. The Gospels, asserts Durant, provide some evidence for the view of Christ as "a social revolutionist." The Apostles "interpreted the Kingdom as a revolutionary inversion of the existing relationships between the rich and the poor; we shall find them and the early Christians forming a communistic band which 'had all things in common.'" Typically, however, Durant doesn't make it that simple, noting that "a conservative can also quote the New Testament to his purpose." The evidence? Christ "uttered no criticism of the civil government, took no known part in the Jewish movement for national liberation, and counseled a submissive gentleness hardly smacking of political revolution." But: "The revolution he sought was a far deeper one, without which reforms could only be superficial and transitory. If he could cleanse the human heart of selfish desire, cruelty, and lust, utopia would come of itself, and all those institutions that rise out of human greed and violence, and the consequent need for law, would disappear." Strong stuff. And: "Since this would be the profoundest of all revolutions, beside which all others would be mere *coups d'etat* of class ousting class and exploiting in its turn," maybe even the "conservative" reading makes Christ "in this spiritual sense the greatest revolutionist in history."[28]

> Christianity arose out of Jewish apocalyptic-esoteric revelations of the coming Kingdom; it derived its impetus from the personality and vision of Christ; it gained strength from the belief in his resurrection, and the promise of eternal life; it received doctrinal form in the theology of Paul; it grew by the absorption of pagan faith and ritual; it became a triumphant Church by inheriting the organizing patterns and genius of Rome.[29]

A good summary, many would feel—though some fundamentalists might be troubled by the emphasis on pagan and Roman elements. And troubled even more by this sentence: "Protestantism was the triumph of Paul over Peter; Fundamentalism is the triumph of Paul over Christ."[30]

In the final analysis, however, Durant is quite willing to assert that "All in all, no more attractive religion [than Christianity] has ever been presented to mankind." His paragraph justifying that assertion emphasizes that it "offered itself without restriction to all individuals, classes, and nations; it was not limited to one people, like Judaism, nor to the freemen of one state, like the official cults of Greece and Rome." He also emphasizes Christianity's tendency toward equality, compassion, hope, forgiveness, brotherhood, kindliness, decency, and peace; but also: "To minds harassed with the insoluble problems of origin and destiny, evil and suffering, it brought a system of divinely revealed doctrine in which the simplest soul could find mental rest."[31] Simplest?

Durant's fourth volume, *The Age of Faith*, is his largest, approaching 1,200 pages; but that is perhaps explained in part by the sub-title: "A History of Medieval Civilization—Christian, Islamic, and Judaic—from Constantine to Dante: A.D. 325-1300." There is much to cover! As the title, *The Age of Faith*, might suggest, the transition from the third volume into this one is smooth. Picking right up on his challenging interpretation of the early church, Durant notes that "for half a century it seemed that Christianity would be Unitarian, and abandon the divinity of Christ." He is referring, of course, to the controversies over the early creeds, many of the doctrines of which, including the trinity, are commonly acknowledged to be non-Biblical. "We cannot interest ourselves today in the many winds of doctrine that agitated the Church in this period," writes Durant; after listing several of the factions, he continues "we can only mourn over the absurdities for which men have died, and will." Discussing Julian the Apostate, who sought to restore paganism as the religion of the land, Durant writes that he gives us "a preview of Higher Criticism" with his insistence that the Gospels "contradict one another, and agree chiefly in their incredibility."[32]

The Arab, suggests Durant, "felt no duty or loyalty to any group larger than his tribe, but the intensity of his devotion varied inversely as its extent; for his tribe he would do with a clear conscience what civilized people do only for their country, religion, or 'race'—i.e., lie, steal, kill, and die." Among the Moslems, Durant continues, "religious ardor declined as wealth grew." Does that make them unique, or is that a pattern? Durant thinks it a pattern—"Faith declines as wealth increases," he writes later in the volume.[33] A "wave of skepticism" arose in the eleventh century, including a sect that "declared all religions false, and laughed at commandments, prayer, fasting, pilgrimage, and alms," and another (under the interesting, seemingly modern name of "Universal Religion") which "deprecated all dogmas, and pled for a purely ethical religion." These latter included agnostics, who held that the doctrines of religion "'may or may not be true; we neither affirm nor deny them, we simply cannot tell; but our consciences will not allow us to accept doctrines whose truth cannot be demonstrated.'"[34]

A chapter on "The Grandeur and Decline of Islam" provides Durant the opportunity to speculate profoundly on the nature of civilization(s) in general, their rise and fall. Despite natural and human-created catastrophes, "the essential processes of civilization are not lost; some younger culture takes them up, snatches them from the conflagration, carries them on imitatively, then creatively, until fresh youth and spirit can enter the race." Civilizations, Durant continues, "are units in a larger whole whose name is history;" civilization is "polygenetic," i.e., it is the co-operative product of many peoples, ranks, and faiths; and no one who studies its history can be a bigot of race or creed." He carries this passionate plea for tolerance and multicultural respect a step further by applying it to the historian: "Therefore the scholar, though he belongs to his country through affectionate kinship, feels himself also a citizen of that Country of the Mind which knows no hatreds and no frontiers; he hardly deserves his name if he carries into his study political prejudices, or racial discriminations, or religious animosities; and he accords his grateful homage to any people that has borne the torch and enriched his heritage."[35] If only the study of the humanities could instill such attitudes in all!

Durant obviously loved the life of the mind. It is, he suggests, "a composition of two forces: the necessity to believe in order to live, and the necessity to reason in order to advance." But: "Beliefs make history, especially when they are wrong; it is for errors that men have most nobly died."[36]

Sometimes Durant seems almost cynical, sarcastic. Of Gregory the Great's writings he wrote: "He left behind him books of popular theology so rich in nonsense that one wonders whether the great administrator believed what he wrote, or merely wrote what he thought it well for simple and sinful souls to believe." Of the Crusades: "Next to the weakening of Christian belief, the chief effects of the Crusades was to stimulate the secular life of Europe by acquaintance with Moslem commerce and industry. War does one good—it teaches people geography."[37] How many American students could locate Afghanistan or Iraq on a world map before the current so-called "war on terrorism"? Sometimes, though, Durant is more direct. "Perhaps he [Gregory VII Hildebrand] had loved righteousness too imperiously, and had hated iniquity too passionately; it is reserved to the philosopher, and forbidden to the man of action, to see elements of justice in the position of his enemy."[38] To see elements of justice in the position of our enemies. What a concept. And what a difficult thing to do!

Consistently, as we have noted, and perhaps especially in this volume on *The Age of Faith*, many of Durant's most insightful and challenging comments deal with religion, which is part of the reason they are emphasized so much here. He characterizes the Middle Ages as "a God-intoxicated age." Do we live in another? Even as he seems to reject the specific beliefs of Christianity, and all religions, Durant is brilliant in recognizing the important role religion plays in the life of a people. The daily hardship, poverty, and grief of Medieval life created a special need for religious faith. "It seemed obvious that the savage impulses of men could be controlled only by a supernaturally sanctioned moral code. . . . The greatest gift of medieval faith was the upholding confidence that right would win in the end, and that every seeming victory of evil would at last be sublimated in the universal triumph of the good." "So the medieval mind, for the most part," Durant concludes later, "surrendered itself to faith, trusted in God and the Church, as modern man trusts in science and the state." Almost always careful, Durant insists that even the excesses of the Christian Inquisition must be seen "against the background of a time accustomed to brutality." Moreover, in our own age (this written in 1950, just after World War II), we have "killed more people in war, and snuffed out more innocent lives without due process of law, than all the wars and persecutions between Caesar and Napoleon." Intolerance, says Durant, is "the natural concomitant of strong faith; tolerance grows only when faith loses certainty; certainty is murderous." Still, even after going to great lengths to help us understand the Inquisition, Durant knows it must be condemned, as must all such extremes. "Making every allowance required of an historian and permitted to a Christian, we must rank the Inquisition, along with the wars and persecutions of our time, as among the darkest blots on the record of mankind, revealing a ferocity unknown in any beast."[39]

Sometimes it does not matter what time or place or subject Durant is dealing with when he gives us his insights; they approach an understanding of human nature itself. People, he suggests, "were no better in the Age of Faith than in our age of doubt, and . . . in all ages law and morality have barely succeeded in maintaining social order against the innate individualism of men never intended by nature to be law-abiding citizens." History, says Durant, perhaps anticipating the so-called "new social history," "always leaves out the average man." And noting the finery that "gentlemen" insisted upon, he concludes that "Those who cater to human vanity seldom starve."[40]

Just a few more insights from Durant's Medieval coverage must satisfy us; mostly these seem to require no comment. The discovery of Medieval Christians that another great faith (Islam) existed with its own great accomplishments was "in itself a disturbing revelation; comparative religion does religion no good." We have spoken of Durant's wit; sometimes it is outright humorous—and even buried in a footnote, as: "Giraldus Cambrensis tells of a youth who, at his father's painful expense, studied philosophy for five years at Paris, and, returning home, proved to his father, by remorseless logic, that the six eggs on the table were twelve; whereupon the father ate the six eggs that he could see, and left the others for his son." Some people are so convinced of their own greatness that they think their works will last forever; one such was this same Cambrensis: "He was sure that his works would immortalize him, but he underestimated the forgetfulness of time." Speaking of the high mortality rate of the Middle Ages (probably less than half of those born reached maturity): "The fertility of women labors to atone for the stupidity of men and the bravery of generals." And finally, in a fitting transition from "medieval" to "modern," Durant concludes with treatment of Dante and writes: "The boundary between 'medieval' and 'modern' is always advancing; and our age of coal and oil and sooty slums may some day be accounted medieval by an era of cleaner power and more gracious life."[41]

As Durant's work moves toward "modern" times, it seems somehow easier to compress our treatment here. Perhaps it is partly that the themes we have noted thus far continue throughout *The Story of Civilization*. In any case, for reasons of space, we must foreshorten our treatment of remaining volumes.

One thing central to Durant's study of *The Renaissance*, of course, is humanism. He seems impressed. The humanists, he writes, "captivated the mind of Italy, turned it from religion to philosophy, from heaven to earth, and revealed to an astonished generation the riches of pagan thought and art. . . . The proper study of mankind was now to be man, in all the potential strength and beauty of his body, in all the joy and pain of his senses and feelings, in all the frail majesty of his reason . . . ." He credits the humanists with revolutionizing the study of history itself; they "ended the succession of medieval chronicles— chaotic and uncritical—by scrutinizing and harmonizing sources, marshaling the matter into order and clarity, vitalizing and humanizing the past by mingling biography with history, and raising their narratives to some level of philosophy by discerning causes, currents, and effects, and studying the regularities and lessons of history." Studying those regularities and lessons of human history is what Durant himself seems to do so well—and what we are trying to do here, through his work. The humanists, certainly, were hard on religion. They "acted as if Christianity were a myth conformable to the needs of popular imagination and morality, but not to be taken seriously by emancipated minds. . . . implicitly they accepted reason as the supreme court . . . . The only immortality they recognized was that which came through the recording of great deeds; they with their pens, not God, would confer it, would destine men to everlasting glory or shame." Their influence "was for a century the dominant factor in the intellectual life of Western Europe."[42] And that influence has lasted.

Not surprisingly, Durant was a product of his time/place/ cultural values, his "climate of opinion," as historians sometimes call it. We all are. We like to think that we are better informed and more sensitive on the subject of homosexuality today than most people were, even Durant, in the 1950s. Two examples must suffice. On Leonardo da Vinci: "Like every artist, every author, and every homosexual, he was unusually self-conscious, sensitive, and vain." And in a description of a painting by Raphael, one figure who appears is "Sappho, too beautiful to be Lesbian . . . ."[43]   Like every homosexual?! Obviously, homosexuals, being human (and constituting, according to most authorities, somewhere between 5 and 10% of the population), reflect the diversity of humanity itself. Too beautiful to be lesbian?! Obviously, again, lesbians mirror the diversity of womankind. Obviously—finally—Durant reflects the predominant attitudes of his time.

Durant's excitement is palpable, and catching, when he writes of Leonardo and the subsequent development of flight:

> Leonardo was on the wrong tack; human flight came not by imitating the bird, except in gliding, but by applying the internal combustion engine to a propellor that could beat the air not downward but backward; forward speed made possible upward flight. But the noblest distinction of man is his passion for knowledge. Shocked by the wars and crimes of mankind, disheartened by the selfishness of ability and the perpetuity of poverty, saddened by the superstitions and credulities with which the nations and generations gild the brevity and indignities of life, we feel our race in some part redeemed when we see that it can hold a soaring dream in its mind and heart for three thousand years, from the legend of Daedalus and Icarus, through the baffled groping of Leonardo and a thousand others, to the glorious and tragic victory of our time.[44]

Despite Leonardo being "on the wrong tack" in terms of flight, Durant praises him highly overall. He was "*the fullest man* of the Renaissance, perhaps of all time. Contemplating his achievement we marvel at the distance that man has come from his origins, and renew our faith in the possibilities of mankind."[45]

Durant is equally glowing in his praise of Michaelangelo, whose *Pieta* earned him this sentence: "In all the history of sculpture no man has ever surpassed it, except, perhaps, the unknown Greek who carved the *Demeter* of the British Museum." Similarly, his ceiling in the Sistine Chapel was "the greatest achievement of any man in the history of painting."[46]

"He put history above philosophy, doubtless feeling that he could learn more about life by studying the record of human behavior than by tracing the web of human theory," Durant wrote of Federigo da Montefeltro.[47] One wonders where Durant himself falls on that spectrum. His doctorate was in philosophy; in *The Story of Civilization*, he is writing history—but with a distinct philosophical orientation. And one wonders where we fall today on that spectrum. Is it cynical to suggest that while we probably value history over philosophy, we fail to appreciate the significance of either adequately?

Though religion does not play as central a role in the Renaissance as in the Middle Ages, some of Durant's greatest insights continue to come in this area. Strong language is used to condemn the church's witchcraft mania: "[I]n Protestant as well as Catholic lands, in the New World as well as the old, burnings for witchcraft were to form the darkest spots in the history of mankind." "Doubtless all religions are based upon assumptions and myths," Durant asserts emphatically; but he follows this with the even more interesting assertion that "these are forgivable if they help to maintain social order and moral discipline." In fairness, it seems he was paraphrasing Francesco Guicciardini when he said that. But this is clearly his own sentiment: "To rulers religion, like almost everything else, is a tool of power." Does it matter what time/place/leader he was discussing when he said that? He was discussing Pope Alexander VI when he wrote, "Like most persons completely orthodox in theology, he was completely worldly in conduct." And discussing two Borgias when he wrote, "The methods used by Alexander and Caesar in realizing [their] aims were those used by all other states then and now—war, diplomacy, deceit, treachery, violation of treaties, and desertion of allies."[48] Perhaps this last is most offensive because the methods in this case were being used by the Papacy, supposedly pledged to the principles of Christ—Durant at least suggests as much. But perhaps the greatest challenge is in asking ourselves to what extent the description applies to our own country's behavior.

Petrarch's warning to Pope Clement VI against trusting physicians deserves quoting at some length. He was filled with "fear," he said, knowing that the Pope's bedside was "beleaguered by doctors," for their "opinions are always conflicting," and "in order to make a name for themselves through some novelty, they traffic with our lives." Even more strongly, he urged the Pope to "look upon their band as an army of enemies," and to remember the epitaph one man had inscribed on his tombstone: "I died of too many physicians." Though Durant follows that quote with the interesting suggestion that "In all civilized lands and times physicians have rivaled women for the distinction of being the most desirable and satirized of mankind,"[49] one cannot help but get the feeling that he shared Petrarch's warning at such length because of its element of truth. Does it hold truth even today?

Durant credits the aforementioned Guicciardini with being "the greatest historian of the sixteenth century," and perhaps to emphasize the importance of great historians, relates how Charles V kept lords and generals waiting while he conversed at length with Guicciardini and justified it by saying, "I can create a hundred nobles in an hour, but I cannot produce such an historian in twenty years."[50]

Durant also quotes Machiavelli at some length on the importance of history: "Wise men say, not without reason, that whoever wishes to foresee the future must consult the past; for human events ever resemble those of preceding times. This arises from the fact that they are produced by men who have been, and ever will be, animated by the same passions; and thus they must necessarily have the same results."[51] Is this stated too strongly, seemingly suggesting that study of the past can *predict* the future? Few professional historians would suggest that to be so. Machiavellianism is perhaps problematic in another way as well. Many of us find ourselves reacting against his purely political point of view, his placing of ethics itself, for example, as subordinate to politics, a mere tool thereof. But perhaps Durant is on target when he suggests: "Philosophers have been well nigh unanimous in condemning *The Prince*, and statesmen in practising its precepts."[52]

"Of course the Renaissance culture was an aristocratic superstructure raised upon the backs of the laboring poor," writes Durant, "but, alas, what culture has not been?"[53] That blunt—painfully true?—insight provides a fitting conclusion for his coverage of the Renaissance. The next "culture" to occupy Durant's attention in *The Story of Civilization* is that of *The Reformation*. Obviously, for much of this sixth volume in the series, religion moves front and center again.

A statement from Durant's preface catches the eye. Noting that he was raised Roman Catholic, spent some years with close ties to Protestantism (particularly Presbyterianism), and had learned a deep appreciation for Judaism, he wrote: "Less than any man have I excuse for prejudice; and I feel for all creeds the warm sympathy of one who has come to learn that even the trust in reason is a precarious faith, and that we are all fragments of darkness groping for the sun. I know no more about the ultimates than the simplest urchin in the streets."[54] But surely he knew more about the approaches of all religions to "the ultimates" than the "simplest urchin" in the street! And his suggestion that "even the trust in reason is a precarious faith" is an interesting one, for it seems clear in his treatment of religion throughout *The Story of Civilization* that reason is exactly where he does place his trust. Most of the time, it serves him well.

Philippe de Comines was considered by Durant to be "the first modern philosophical historian," for "he seeks the relations of cause and effect, analyzes character, motives, and pretenses, judges conduct objectively, and studies events and original documents to illuminate the nature of man and the state." Is it surprising that after taking that approach to the past, Comines also had a "pessimistic estimate of mankind"?[55]

Teachers of the humanities often find one of their greatest challenges is helping students understand what things were like *before* important developments that they take for granted. There is that built-in tendency, it appears, to assume that the reality we know is the way it has always been. How hard is it for us, and our students, to feature what it was like before the printing press? "To describe all its effects," suggests Durant, "would be to chronicle half the history of the modern mind." A few examples: "[I]t paved the way for the Enlightenment, for the American and French revolutions, for democracy." But typically Durant: "And, after speech, it provided a readier instrument for the dissemination of nonsense than the world has ever known until our time."[56]

Durant would never justify something like the Spanish Inquisition, with its persecution and torture of those with different religious beliefs, but not surprisingly, he is helpful in understanding how such extreme intolerance can develop. For people in those days, he suggests, their theologies were their "most prized and confident possessions; and they looked upon those who rejected these creeds as attacking the foundations of social order and the very significance of human life. Each group was hardened by certainty into intolerance, and branded the others as infidels." "Hardened by certainty into intolerance"—a painful truth! "Our present intolerance," Durant insists, providing perspective and keeping us from being too comfortable in condemning those of the past, "is rather for those who question our economic or political principles . . . ." More specifically, writing in 1957 as the Communist witch-hunting of McCarthyism was going on, Durant writes that "Both the Inquisition and the witch-burning were expressions of an age afflicted with homicidal certainty in theology, as the patriotic massacres of our era may be due in part to homicidal certainty in ethnic or political theory." Finally, we must "try to understand such movements [as the Inquisition] in terms of their time," though they "seem to us now the most unforgivable of historic crimes." He concludes pungently that "A supreme and unchallengeable faith is a deadly enemy to the human mind."[57]

Sometimes Durant's admiration of figures is obvious, as with Erasmus, who considered nationalism a curse to humanity and challenged statesmen to forge a universal state. "I wish to be called a citizen of the world," said Erasmus in a generally nationalistic world, and "The most sublime thing is to deserve well of the human race."[58] Surely a needed perspective in any age.

Durant is not always gentle with the great leaders of the Protestant Reformation such as Martin Luther. Though acknowledging that "we may rank Luther with Copernicus, Voltaire, and Darwin as the most powerful personalities in the modern world," Durant also writes of Luther that "He freed his followers from an infallible pope, but subjected them to an infallible book; and it has been easier to change the popes than the book." Durant is also especially critical of Luther for his anti-Jewish utterances, suggesting that "They set the tone in Germany for centuries, and prepared its people for genocidal holocausts." Another great Reformation figure, John Calvin, "was as thorough as any pope in rejecting individualism of belief; this greatest legislator of Protestantism completely repudiated that principle of private judgment with which the new religion had begun." And, even more harshly, "we shall always find it hard to love the man who darkened the human soul with the most absurd and blasphemous conception of God in all the long and honored history of nonsense."[59]

Such harsh judgment is not reserved for religious leaders alone; Russia's Ivan the Terrible elicits this sentence from Durant: "He was one of the many men of his time of whom it might be said that it would have been better for their country and humanity if they had never been born."[60]

In another passage, Durant perhaps can be said to foresee the so-called new social history. "What, after all, were the bulls and blasts of popes and Protestants, the rival absurdities of murderous mythologies, the strut and succession, gout and syphilis, of emperors and kings, compared with the inexorable struggle for food, shelter, clothing, health, mates, children, life?" "Civilization," Durant suggests, might even be seen from this perspective as "a parasite on the man with the hoe."[61] He even entitles this chapter "The Life of the People, 1517—64," hinting at the later-popular label for the concern with the lives of the masses of the people, "people's history."

Occasionally, someone still drags out the prophecies of Nostrodamus as if they have legitimacy; they should read Durant, who notes that Nostrodamus prophesied a life of ninety years for Charles IX—who died ten years later at the age of twenty-four. Durant concludes that Nostrodamus at his own death in 1566 "left a book of prophecies so wisely ambiguous that some line or another could be applied to almost any event in later history."[62]

Occasionally Durant's ability to step outside the mainstream of his time is remarkable. Surely not many would have written in 1957 of the Spanish conquest of America that "there is little doubt that the conquered were at the time more civilized than their actual conquerors."[63]

Appropriately, Durant ends his coverage of *The Reformation* with an emphasis on the importance of tolerance. "The greatest gift of the Reformation," he insists, "was to provide Europe and America with that competition of faiths which puts each on its mettle, cautions it to tolerance, and gives to our frail minds the zest and test of freedom." For "One lesson emerges above the smoke of the battle: a religion is at its best when it must live with competition; it tends to intolerance when and where it is unchallenged and supreme."

But Durant also ends this volume with "COURAGE, READER: WE NEAR THE END."[64]

In this case, he lied. Well, at least he was wrong. His anticipated five-volume series was to extend to eleven. The seventh was *The Age of Reason Begins*, which covered the period 1558-1648; significantly, the people mentioned in his sub-title were Shakespeare, Bacon, Montaigne, Rembrandt, Galileo, and Descartes. "In this period," Durant wrote, "the basic developments were the rise of murderous nationalisms and the decline of murderous theologies." True, but it should be noted also that the focus of this volume is even more on cultural history than in previous ones. Finally, it should be noted that, as Durant puts it, "Mrs. Durant's part in these concluding volumes has been so substantial that our names must be united on the title page."[65] And so it was done; on volumes 7-11, the title page carries "Will and Ariel Durant" as co-authors; this seventh they dedicated "To Our Beloved Daughter, Ethel."

"The past is helpless in the hands of the present, which repeatedly remolds it to the hour's whim," the Durants write, in a confession interesting for any historian.[66] Perhaps they were responding in part to the changing "climate of opinion" of the 1960s; this was the first volume of *The Story of Civilization* to appear in that decade. But they also insist that "History smiles at all attempts to force its flow into theoretical patterns or logical grooves; it plays havoc with our generalizations, breaks all our rules. History is baroque."[67]

The terrorist attacks on the United States on September 11, 2001, color our reading of everything, including the Durants. Here, at some length, is the conclusion of their chapter entitled "The Islamic Challenge, 1566-1648:"

> Such was Persia, such was Islam, in this last flowering of their power and art—a civilization profoundly unlike ours of the West, and at times contemptuously hostile, denouncing us as polytheists and materialists, laughing at our matriarchal monogamy, and sometimes coming in avalanches to batter down our gates; we could not be expected to understand it, or admire

its art, when the great debate was between Moslem and Christian, not yet between Darwin and Christ. The competition of the cultures is not over, but for the most part it has ceased to shed blood, and they are now free to mingle in the osmosis of mutual influence. The East takes on our industries and armaments and becomes Western, the West wearies of wealth and war and seeks inner peace. Perhaps we shall help the East to mitigate poverty and superstition, and the East will help us to humility in philosophy and refinement in art. East is West and West is East, and soon the twain will meet.[68]

In this post-9-11 world, can that be helpful in discussion with your students? And can these words of John Comenius, themselves written in the 1600s, help?

We are all citizens of one world, we are all of one blood. To hate a man because he was born in another country, because he speaks a different language, or because he takes a different view on this subject or that, is a great folly. Desist, I implore you, for we are all equally human. . . . Let us have but one end in view, the welfare of humanity; and let us put aside all selfishness in considerations of language, nationality, or religion.[69]

The final pages of *The Age of Reason Begins* returns to related themes, themes often returned to by the Durants. Galileo, while promising submission to the church as he explored new scientific theories, also said that he "did not feel obliged to believe that that same God who has endowed us with sense, reason, and intellect has intended us to forgo their use." And the Durants, while acknowledging that "the soul of a civilization is its religion," also insist that "Religion was a casualty in the wars of religion."[70]

The eighth volume of *The Story of Civilization* carries the full title, *The Age of Louis XIV: A History of European Civilization in the Period of Pascal, Moliere, Cromwell, Milton, Peter the Great, Newton, and Spinoza: 1648-1715*. The Durants, in their "Dear Reader" note at the beginning of the volume, admitted that "This volume is Part VIII in a history whose beginning has been forgotten, and whose end we shall never reach." It was 1963. After describing their plans for completing the series, or at least getting as close to doing so as they could, they showed their awareness of current events, specifically the Cold War, by writing, "Meanwhile we shall rely on the Great Powers not to destroy our subject before it destroys us."[71] By now, the dedication was to their granddaughter.

"The historian, like the journalist, tends to lose the normal background of an age in the dramatic foreground of his picture, for he knows that his readers will relish the exceptional and will wish to personify processes and events."[72] Indeed, how often—especially as history was traditionally done, before the advent of so-called "people's history," of which the Durants sometimes seem pioneers—have we lost the "background" by focusing too exclusively on the "dramatic foreground?" Our students must have often thought, "Okay, I get it, history is the story of presidents, kings, queens, generals, rich people," and equally often wondered, "Where are we the people in history?"

Sometimes the comments of the Durants seem to require no comment here—or is that only because we must hurry toward a conclusion?—yet are profound, simple, humorous, or more. Noting that not many read John Milton's masterpiece "Paradise Lost" today: "We have so little leisure now that we have invented so many labor-saving devices." Still on Milton, and noting that he has even Satan making speeches: "It is disturbing to learn that even in hell we shall have to listen to lectures." (Many of our students should love that!) Describing King Charles II of England as a deist, then explaining: "i. e., one who acknowledged a Supreme Being, more or less impersonal, and interpreted the remainder of the religious creeds as popular poetry." (Deism, of course, was to play a crucial role in American history, especially among the Revolutionary generation, the Founding Fathers.) Describing the relationship between different disciplines: "History is a fragment of biology—the human moment in the pageant of species. It is also a child of geography—the operation of land and sea and air, and of their forms and products, upon human desire and destiny." And after quoting Henry Oldenburg —"I hope that in time all nations, even the less civilized, will embrace each other as dear comrades, and will join forces, both intellectual and material, to banish ignorance and to make true and useful philosophy regnant"—concluding: "It is still the hope of the world."[73]

Assessing the thought of Pierre Bayle, sometimes considered the "Father of the Enlightenment," the Durants seem to agree with him, and, as ever, are thoughtful on the role of religion in society. Bayle dealt "boldly" with "one of the most difficult problems of history," i. e., can a moral code be maintained without the aid of supernatural belief? Noting the crime, corruption, and immorality prevalent in supposedly Christian Europe—and among the Jews and Muslims as well—Bayle decided that apparently religious belief has little influence on conduct, that a society of atheists would likely have no worse morals than a society of Christians. What keeps most of us in order is not "the distant and uncertain terror of hell," but "the fear of the policeman and the law, of social condemnation and disgrace, of the hangman." The words are the Durants' rather than Bayle's, and they do go on—typically, rather than leaving it so simple—to admonish him a bit: "Whether the morals of the average man would be worse than they are if religion did not supplement law is a question that Bayle leaves untouched."[74]

Will Durant always loved philosophy, and Spinoza was clearly one of his favorite philosophers. The Durants credit him here with being the person who made "the boldest attempt in modern history to find a philosophy that could take the place of a lost religious faith." After summarizing Spinoza's critique of the Bible, they quote him as saying it is a sufficient creed to believe in "a God, that is, a supreme being who loves justice and charity," and whose proper worship "consists in the practice of justice and love towards one's neighbor." Then their own words: "No other doctrine is necessary."[75]

The ninth volume, *The Age of Voltaire*, is massive. But we must restrain ourselves; besides, most of the important themes are evident by now, have been illustrated with several examples. Still, a few cannot be resisted. "Brutal punishments, administered in public, encouraged public brutality." "History is philosophy teaching by examples," wrote Henry St. John Bolingbroke.[76] Clearly, the Durants agreed; clearly, the Durants' history can be used for that purpose!

Voltaire's words on religion and tolerance are famous: "If one religion only were allowed in England, the government would very possibly become arbitrary; if there were but two, the people would cut one another's throats; but as there is such a multitude, they all live happy and in peace."[77] Many would suggest that goes a long way toward explaining the growth of religious toleration and freedom in the United States, where we have developed hundreds of different approaches to Christianity alone.

The debt we owe to Voltaire, especially his historical work, the Durants make clear by a question: "And what are we doing here but walking in the path of Voltaire?"[78] And what are we doing here but walking in the path of Will and Ariel Durant?

Their explanation of natural/supernatural seems common sense: "When novel situations and events did not readily lend themselves to natural explanations, the common mind ascribed them to supernatural causes, and rested."[79] Yet will such an assertion not be controversial in many circles even today? Similarly, on the relationship between religion and science: "The growth of science . . . is the positive side of that basic modern development whose negative side is the decline of supernatural belief." In effect, "Two priesthoods came into conflict: the one devoted to the molding of character through religion, the other to the education of the intellect through science." And finally: "The first priesthood predominates in ages of poverty or disaster, when men are grateful for spiritual comfort and moral order; the second in ages of progressive wealth, when men incline to limit their hopes to the earth."[80]

And speaking of priesthood—the story of the atheist French priest Jean Meslier is a powerful one, whatever one's religious persuasion: "Picture the lonely priest, shorn of all faith and hope, living out his silenced life in a village where probably every soul but his own would have been horrified to learn his secret thoughts."[81]

The Durants speak of "the fascination of philosophy—which draws us ever onward because it never answers the questions that we never cease to ask."[82] But isn't that exactly what some find so frustrating about it? Those who do probably long for the certainty of religion instead.

Speaking of Diderot: "Like all of us, he grew more conservative as his years and his income increased."[83] Is it true? Not of Diderot, so much, but is it true in general? And how can our young students know?

In a chapter entitled "The Triumph of the *Philosophes*, 1715-89," the Durants assert that "when a religion consents to reason it begins to die."[84] Is that true?

The Age of Voltaire concludes with a lengthy "Epilogue in Elysium," the kind of thing that drives most mainstream historians bonkers—an imaginary conversation between Pope Benedict XIV and Voltaire! Two brief quotations must suffice. When Voltaire suggests that "reason is the noblest gift that God has given us," the Pope replies "No; love is. I do not wish to belittle reason, but it should be the servant of love, not of pride." And when Voltaire suggests that the reason for the growth of the church is the Pope's "devilishly subtle encouragement of fertility," the Pope insists, of course, that that is not the case. "Shall I tell you why intelligent people all over the world are returning to religion?" he asks. Voltaire responds bluntly "Because they are tired of thinking." Again, the Pope objects. "Not quite," he insists. "They have discovered that your philosophy has no answer but ignorance and despair."[85] Probably we can agree that the big, important questions are fated to be debated forever; but even in Heaven?

Does the aging of the Durants themselves have something to do with the recurrence of the theme of increased conservatism with age? Early on in their tenth volume, *Rousseau and Revolution,* and speaking of Rousseau, they write: "We must allow for development: a man's ideas are a function of his experience and his years; it is natural for a thinking person to be an individualist in youth—loving liberty and grasping for ideals—and a moderate in maturity, loving order and reconciled to the possible."[86] Again, is this true? One hears much of the conservatism of youth today.

"Ferocity of punishment breeds ferocity of character, even in the non-criminal public,"[87] assert the Durants, paraphrasing Beccaria. Could this simple statement serve as a good basis for a discussion of the legitimacy of the death penalty?

Germany's Frederick was insightful on history; he included that it was an excellent teacher, but with few pupils. "It is in the nature of man that no one learns from experience," he insisted. "The follies of the fathers are lost on their children; each generation has to commit its own."[88] Must it always be so? Must history constantly repeat itself because no one was listening the first time? Then why do we study history?

"To Voltaire, more than to any other individual, we owe the religious toleration that now precariously prevails in Europe and North America,"[89] assert the Durants. Is it perhaps even more precarious today than when they wrote in the 1960s?

And speaking of religious toleration. Can we respect an individual for having the courage of his or her convictions, for standing up for them even unto death, even as we might condemn their specific views? The Durants relate that Diderot, near death, was visited by a priest, the same one who had visited Voltaire near his end. The priest begged Diderot to return to the church, and warned him that unless he received the sacraments he could not enjoy burial in a cemetery. Diderot reportedly replied "I understand you, Monsieur le Cure. You refused to bury Voltaire because he did not believe in the divinity of the Son. Well, when I am dead, they can bury me wherever they like, but I declare that I believe neither in the Father nor in the Holy Ghost, nor in any of the Family."[90]

"So we end our survey, in these last two volumes, of the century whose conflicts and achievements are still active in the life of mankind today."[91] So asserted the Durants in an "Envoi" at the end of this tenth volume. And it is, of course, part of our contention that not just the conflicts and achievements covered by the Durants' last two volumes but the conflicts and achievements of the entire span of the story of civilization do indeed live on for us today. But the Durants were wrong in their assertion nonetheless, for the series initially projected as five volumes did not even manage to end with ten; rather, after an eight-year hiatus, the Durants could not resist publishing one more, *The Age of Napoleon*. They explained in their Preface that "the Reaper repeatedly overlooked us," so that they grew weary of their "insipid and unaccustomed leisure." So, "To give our days some purpose and program we decided to apply to the age of Napoleon (1789-1815) our favorite method of integral history —weaving into one narrative all memorable aspects of European civilization in those twenty-seven years: statesmanship, war, economics, morals, manners, religion, science, medicine, philosophy, literature, drama, music, and art; to see them all as elements in one moving picture, and as interacting parts of a united whole."[92] And all of those elements are indeed present, as with all of the volumes in the massive series. But many critics felt, with some cause, that the Durants were no longer as effective.

Still, there are some lessons, some food for thought and discussion—some examples of wit and wisdom—worthy of brief note here. Though, not surprisingly by this point, they relate to themes already considered. Movingly, thoughtfully, the Durants include in their acknowledgments this statement, something of an affirmation of faith in the human race: "All in all, in life and history, we have found so many good men and women that we have quite lost faith in the wickedness of mankind."[93]

Religion, as ever, is a persistent theme here. What is its role in civilization? And here, at the end of the story of civilization, further thoughts about its role in morality, and in politics. Quoting the Directory's edict to teachers, "You must exclude from your teaching all that relates to the dogmas or rites of any religion or sect whatever. . . [T]he teaching of them is not part of public instruction, nor can it ever be," the Durants note: "Here, clearly put, was one of the most difficult enterprises of the Revolution, as it is one of the difficult problems of our time: to build a social order upon a system of morality independent of religious belief. Napoleon was to judge the proposal impracticable; America was to cleave to it till our time."[94] Those words were written in 1975; one wonders, does America still cleave to it? And how hard is it to teach religion as a part of history (which it clearly is—history without it is indisputably incomplete) without teaching religion? "The twentieth century approaches its end without having yet found a natural substitute for religion in persuading the human animal to morality,"[95] assert the Durants. But is it unfair to take note also of the massive persecution and killing in the name of religion throughout history—and today?

Appropriately, in a volume on *The Age of Napoleon*, Napoleon himself is helpful. On history (and philosophy): "My son should study much history, and meditate upon it, for it is the only true philosophy." Helpful too on religion. Though he lost his religious faith at the age of thirteen, the Durants note that "Sometimes he wished he had kept it," and quote him saying "I imagine it must give great and true happiness." In a famous story, Napoleon is with some skeptical scientists in Egypt, and challenges them, "You may talk as long as you please, gentlemen, but who made all that?" He reportedly pointed at the stars. Speaking now of evolving religious faith, the Durants once again suggest things change as we age. "[W]hat thoughtful person has not at fifty discarded the dogmas he swore by in his youth, and will not at eighty smile at the 'mature' views of his middle age?"[96] Perhaps so; at least, shouldn't the possibility promote tolerance?

Let the great Chateaubriand have the final word. For it is a final word about the nature of history itself—which is really our subject here, is it not? The words are actually those of the Durants, paraphrasing Chateaubriand: "History is a circle, or an enlarged repetition of the same circle, with frills that make the old seem new; the same good and the same evil survive in men despite such mighty overturns [as revolutions]. There is no real progress; knowledge grows, but merely to serve instincts that do not change."[97] At least there is that to hold onto: knowledge grows. And surely it is evident by now that Will and Ariel Durant can help it to do so!

What the Durants called their "integrated history" approach seems a powerful tool for understanding, applicable to varied disciplines, which is rare in our day of extreme specialization. I was talking about this, which is part of the appeal of "Durant" to me, with a friend. Specialization, he suggested, is like sitting outside in a beautiful setting (flowers, trees, stars) and illuminating with a flashlight only one limb of one tree—thus missing the holistic view, the *beauty* of the whole scene.[98] The Durants help us see the whole scene.

The friend to whom this long survey (but small compared to the magnitude of *The Story of Civilization*!) is dedicated used to like to begin the required survey course in United States history by telling his students that he would insult their country, their religion, their Mother. That was his way of saying that part of the job of a university professor is to grab people and shake them and make them think. Again, the wisdom (and wit) of Will (and

Ariel) Durant in *The Story of Civilization* provide a valuable tool for that process, some possible lessons for teachers and students.

Another reader of the series would surely choose different lessons to emphasize from those chosen here. The Durants themselves published a volume as they neared the end of the series entitled specifically *The Lessons of History*,[99] which we have chosen to ignore here in order to emphasize some of our own favorites. That's the basic point—the series is a rich resource for any who would ponder the wisdom of the past.

1. Will Durant, *Heroes of History: A Brief History of Civilization from Ancient Times to the Dawn of the Modern Age* (New York: Simon and Schuster, 2001), p. 76.

2. Will Durant, *The Story of Civilization: Volume 1: Our Oriental Heritage* (New York: Simon and Schuster, 1935), pp. vii and x.

3. New York: W. W. Norton & Co.

4. Durant, *Our Oriental Heritage*, pp. 1-2.

5. *Ibid.*, p. 4.

6. *Ibid.*, p. 5.

7. *Ibid.*, p. 7.

8. *Ibid.*, pp. 66, 71, and 86.

9. *Ibid.*, p. 99.

10. *Ibid.*, p. 134.

11. *Ibid.*, p. 140.

12. *Ibid.*, pp. 146, 153, 159, 171, 175, and 178.

13. *Ibid.*, p. 244.

14. *Ibid.*, pp. 369, 381, 360, and 382.

15. *Ibid.*, pp. 407 and 394.

16. *Ibid.*, pp. 414-415, 633, 463, and 525.

17. *Ibid.*, pp. 422 and 449.

18. *Ibid.*, p. 759.

19. *Ibid.*, pp. 829 and 845.

20. Will Durant, *The Story of Civilization: Volume 2: The Life of Greece* (New York: Simon and Schuster, 1939), pp. 96, 295, 565, and 578.

21. *Ibid.*, pp. 428-429 and 513.

22. *Ibid.*, p. 534.

23. *Ibid.*, pp. 587 and 633.

24 Will Durant, *The Story of Civilization: Volume 3: Caesar and Christ* (New York: Simon and Schuster, 1944), pp. 79, 149, and 245.

25. *Ibid.*, p. 434.

26. *Ibid.*, p. 472.

27. *Ibid.*, pp. 484 and 489.

28. *Ibid.*, pp. 565-566.

29. *Ibid.*, p. 575.

30. *Ibid.*, p. 592.

31. *Ibid.*, p. 602.

32. Will Durant, *The Story of Civilization: Volume 4: The Age of Faith* (New York: Simon and Schuster, 1950), pp. 8, 47, and 15.

33. *Ibid.*, pp. 157, 301, and 710.

34. *Ibid.*, p. 301.

35. *Ibid.*, pp. 343-344.

36. *Ibid.*, pp. 405 and 458.

37. *Ibid.*, pp. 522 and 612.

38. *Ibid.*, p. 551.

39. *Ibid.*, pp. 732, 737-738, and 784.

40. *Ibid.*, pp. 829, 843, and 849.

41. *Ibid.*, pp. 955, 982, 992, 1003, and 1082.

42. Will Durant, *The Story of Civilization: Volume 5: The Renaissance* (New York: Simon and Schuster, 1953), pp. 77-85.

43. *Ibid.*, pp. 216 and 460.

44. *Ibid.*, p. 221.

45 *Ibid.*, pp. 227-228.

46. *Ibid.*, pp. 467 and 475.

47. *Ibid.*, p. 342.

48. *Ibid.*, pp. 528, 545-546, 410, 413, and 436.

49. *Ibid.*, p. 531.

50. *Ibid.*, p. 545.

51. *Ibid.*, p. 555.

52. *Ibid.*, p. 564.

53. *Ibid.*, p. 726.

54. Will Durant, *The Story of Civilization: Volume 6: The Reformation* (New York: Simon and Schuster, 1957), p. viii.

55. *Ibid.*, p. 100.

56. *Ibid.*, pp. 159-160.

57. *Ibid.*, pp. 208, 216.

58. *Ibid.*, pp. 287-288.

59. *Ibid.*, pp. 452, 473, 727, and 490.

60. *Ibid.*, p. 662.

61. *Ibid.*, pp. 751-752.

62. *Ibid.*, p. 851.

63. *Ibid.*, p. 864.

64. *Ibid.*, p. 940.

65. Will and Ariel Durant, *The Story of Civilization: Volume 7: The Age of Reason Begins* (New York: Simon and Schuster, 1961), pp. vii-viii.

66. *Ibid.*, p. 93.

67. *Ibid.*, p. 267.

68 *Ibid.*, pp. 536-537.

69. *Ibid.*, p. 582.

70. *Ibid.*, pp. 607, 613, and 614.

71. Will and Ariel Durant, *The Story of Civilization: Volume 8: The Age of Louis XIV* (New York: Simon and Schuster, 1963), p. vii.

72. *Ibid.*, p. 46.

73. *Ibid.*, pp. 235, 238, 251, 365, and 498.

74. *Ibid.*, pp. 606-607.

75. *Ibid.*, pp. 620 and 627.

76. Will and Ariel Durant, *The Story of Civilization: Volume 9: The Age of Voltaire* (New York: Simon and Schuster, 1965), pp 69 and 100.

77. *Ibid.*, p. 119.

78. *Ibid.*, p. 489.

79. *Ibid.*, p. 493.

80. *Ibid.*, p. 507.

81. *Ibid.*, p. 617.

82. *Ibid.*, p. 624.

83. *Ibid.*, p. 666.

84. *Ibid.*, p. 755.

85. *Ibid.*, pp. 789-790.

86. Will and Ariel Durant, *The Story of Civilization: Volume 10: Rousseau and Revolution* (New York: Simon and Schuster, 1967), pp. 177-178.

87. *Ibid.*, p. 320.

88. *Ibid.*, p. 529.

89. *Ibid.*, p. 881.

90 *Ibid.*, p. 893.

91. *Ibid.*, p. 964.

92. Will and Ariel Durant, *The Story of Civilization: Volume 11: The Age of Napoleon* (New York: Simon and Schuster, 1975), p. vii.

93. *Ibid.*, p. ix.

94. *Ibid.*, p. 127.

95. *Ibid.*, p. 154.

96. *Ibid.*, pp. 253-254.

97. *Ibid.*, p. 312.

98. Thanks, Bill Fredrick!

99. Will and Ariel Durant, *The Lessons of History* (New York: Simon and Schuster, 1968).

CHAPTER 8

A Relevant Religion

If you read the previous chapter, you know that one of the central themes of the Durants' *Story of Civilization* is religion. It's one of the central themes of my life as well. I'm a Unitarian Universalist. I discovered that faith, specifically the Unitarian part, through my study of history—I remember being impressed at William Ellery Channing's condemnation of slavery from the pulpit, and he's considered the founder of American Unitarianism. You see, I have found that I cannot separate my life into neat compartments anymore, indeed don't wish to try. Howard Zinn helped teach me that in terms of the classroom and the so-called "real world." More broadly, for me, it also includes religion. The Native American peoples had it right. I'm told that none of their languages included a word that translated into English as "religion." But that does not mean that they were not deeply religious, just that they didn't separate it out from the rest of their lives. In other words, it wasn't something you said you believe, or something you do one day a week, but rather a vital part of how you live your life. So, as noted, I discovered my Unitarian Universalist faith through my study of history, and that faith informs my understanding of history—and the world. I find it a relevant religion. This chapter is an attempt to explain and illustrate that.

There's a contest of sorts going on as I write this in which the Unitarian Universalist Association has solicited "Elevator Speeches," in other words, brief responses to the question "What's a Unitarian Universalist?" Here's the one I've submitted:

> Unitarianism was a version of Christianity that rejected the trinity, Universalism a version of Christianity that believed all human souls would ultimately be reconciled to God. But these days, UUs are far more, ranging from atheist to Christian. What ties them together? They believe in a FREE FAITH, one that has no creedal test, one that emphasizes freedom of belief, reason as the best tool we have to figure out what to believe, and toleration of a broad diversity of beliefs. What All Souls Unitarian Church of Tulsa, Oklahoma, does for me is to provide me with a supportive religious community that challenges me to work out—and, most importantly, live out—my own beliefs, rather than telling me what I have to believe. Oops . . . the elevator just stopped . . .

I don't know if my "Elevator Speech" will be selected, but I'm comfortable enough with it, especially with its emphasis on *living out* one's religion. I'm not much interested in arguing about theology, but more interested in what you do to make the world a better place, and I'd argue that's what a guy named Jesus taught some 2,000 years ago.

The most important minister in my life has been The Rev. John B. Wolf, who both influenced me theologically and helped me through a hard time in my life with his pastoral counseling. I remember many times hearing John remind us that one of the root words of religion is *religio*, suggesting to bind together. How ironic, then, and tragic, that religion so often divides people, to the point that we can actually believe God is on our side as we kill people in his/her/its name.

As a long-time member of All Souls (since 1967), and, I'm sure, as a professional historian, I was the one asked to edit a new history of the church, which is forthcoming as I write this. In that history, one of the things I did was put together a series on "Theological Diversity at All Souls." This is my introduction to that series.

☮

It should come as no surprise that a church without a creed, which emphasizes freedom, reason, and toleration as basic principles, would incorporate a lot of different theological positions. And All Souls does! (Our Minister Emeritus, The Rev. John B. Wolf, once entitled a book, *The Gift of Doubt.* I don't know about you, but in the churches in which I grew up, doubt was not a gift but a sin.) Herewith we present a series expressing some of the many different theologies that exist in our church. This is consistent with what's going on in our *UU World* magazine. A recent issue had carried an essay on humanistic religious naturalism. Spring '07 carried a piece on gratitude rooted in a doctrine of God. The next issue was to feature Buddhist ideas and practices within Unitarian Universalism. Our faith is obviously a diverse one, and has no "official theology."

When I was discussing UU theological diversity with our Senior Minister, The Rev. Marlin Lavanhar, he was very supportive, but with a cautionary note. He advised that we not give the impression that we are equally divided between different belief systems. Theologically, most of us are probably somewhere between liberal Christian and religious humanist. Or, as Rev. Lavanhar said on another occasion, "the core is liberal Christian, Judaism, and humanism....there is considerable interest in Eastern religious ideas and practices in our ranks dating back to Unitarian minister Ralph Waldo Emerson, who introduced Transcendentalism into our faith in the early 19th century." It also seems appropriate to note that the Unitarian Universalist Association lists many sources for our religious tradition, including the world's religions, and more specifically Jewish, Christian, and humanist teachings, as well as Earth-centered traditions.

Kathy Keith, our Executive Director, has been doing an excellent series in *Simple Gifts* [a monthly newsletter of the church] called "A Mighty Cloud of Witnesses," about some important individuals in the life of All Souls over the years. Let's consider this sort of "a mighty cloud of contemporary/diverse/ theological witnesses."

Several of these essays have already seen print in *Simple Gifts* over the past few months. But this group by no means exhausts all the possibilities. What's *your* theology? For part of the purpose of a series such as this is to help you engage in the on-going process of working on your own theology—just as All Souls continues to evolve over its 85 years!

☮

In the series, I used essays by church members on an incredible array of theological positions, including agnostic, Unitarian Universalist Christian, humanist, religious humanist, panentheist, Buddhist, and Earth-Centered Spirituality. (The humanist and religious humanist essays, by the way, were written by a husband and wife!) And finally, I wrote an essay for the series myself, on Unitarian Universalism—here it is.

☮

It might seem strange that Unitarian Universalism should be just one of many different theological positions at our church— after all, it is All Souls Unitarian Church. But as noted in the introduction to this series, a non-creedal church, in which we are FREE to use our REASON to work out our own beliefs as long as we TOLERATE others, does incorporate lots of diversity. My personal theology is Unitarian Universalism.

Originally, it seems clear to me, Christianity was neither Trinitarian nor Unitarian. The church conferences of the 4th century spelled out the Trinity, and by definition those who did not believe that way were Unitarians. They were also persecuted. But if I am a Christian, I am a Unitarian Christian; as it says in stone above the door of every Unitarian church I saw in Hungary and Romania, "God is One" (or "There is only one God").

Universalists insisted over the centuries that their God is a God of love, that if there's such a place as hell, ultimately no-one will be there, because God's love is all-inclusive. If I am a Christian, I am a Universalist Christian.

What excites me about All Souls is that there is no creed that I am told I have to believe in. Instead, I find a supportive religious community in which I am challenged to work out—and live out!—my own religious beliefs. The "live out" part is very important; as my wife, Carole, said in a recent talk to the Evening Alliance, when Religion in Action came up, "What other way is there for religion to be?"

It is not true, as some of our critics would have it, that we believe nothing. And it is not true that we are free to believe anything. Most of us, for example, would insist that our beliefs meet the test of human reason. And we, Unitarian Universalists, do have Principles. Seven of them: "the inherent worth and dignity of every person; justice, equity and compassion in human relations; acceptance of one another and encouragement to spiritual growth in our congregations; a free and responsible search for truth and meaning; the right of conscience and the use of the democratic process within our congregations and in society at large; the goal of world community with peace, liberty and justice for all; respect for the interdependent web of all existence of which we are a part." Not bad for the heart of a religion, in my view. The Rev. John B. Wolf used to remind us that religion was supposed to bind us together; those seven principles seem to me a good start.

Here, in our congregation, we have certain things that serve that same purpose. Like our Covenant that we speak together every Sunday: "Love is the Spirit of this Church; and Service is its Law. This is our Great Covenant: To dwell together in peace, to seek the truth in love, and to help one another." As The Rev. Gerald Davis of Church of the Restoration would say, "And the church was heard to say 'Amen.'"

And the statement on the back of our Sunday morning service each week: "This church is dedicated to religion but not to creed. Neither upon itself nor upon its members does it impose a test of doctrinal formulas. It regards love of God and humankind and the perfecting of our spiritual nature as the unchanging substance of religion and the essential gospel of Jesus. Consecrating itself to these principles, it aims at cultivating reverence for truth, moral character, and insight, helpfulness to humanity, and the spirit of communion with the infinite. It welcomes to its worship and fellowship all who are in sympathy with a religion thus simple and free." Again, I say "Amen!"

A "good religion," it seems to me, is one which sustains you, fulfills you, makes you a better person. Being a Southern Baptist has done that for my Mother for 92 years. I believe/hope/pray that being a Unitarian Universalist does it for me.

I am a Unitarian Universalist. All Souls Unitarian Church is where I practice my faith.

I have made much here of religion not being separate from the rest of our lives. Let me illustrate. Our church has a series of monthly themes throughout the year; essentially, everything that goes on, in religious education classes, worship services, etc., relates to the monthly theme. You will find it significant, perhaps, that some of those themes over the past few years have been democracy, freedom, peace—not necessarily things you would hear a lot about in some churches. I was honored to be called on to write an essay on the theme of democracy in the November, 2004, issue of *Simple Gifts*. Here it is.

Have you ever noticed that there are certain words everyone uses, seemingly based on the assumption that we all know what they mean and that we all mean the same thing by them, but it's not necessarily the case? Like "liberal." How in the world did it happen that "liberal" became a dirty word in American politics, so that even some people who are don't feel free to say so? My dictionary tells me "liberal" means "favorable to progress or reform." Other words that show up in definitions include "of or pertaining to representational forms of government rather than aristocracies and monarchies," "maximum individual freedom," "governmental protection of civil liberties," "tolerant," "free," "generous."

The dictionary is not a bad place to start for "democracy," either; indeed, I would argue, the two, liberal and democracy, are not unrelated. Democracy is "a form of government in which the supreme power is vested in the people and exercised directly by them or by their elected agents under a free electoral system." (Also: "formal equality of rights and privileges," "the common people of a community as distinguished from any privileged class.")

But surely Abraham Lincoln stated the essence of democracy best—"government of the people, by the people, for the people." (Abraham Lincoln said so many things best!)

I'm an American historian, so I think historically about any topic, including democracy. What I see when I look back at our history is a slow, painful, still-incomplete growth of democracy. Many people coming to America were seeking greater freedom, economic/religious/political. The Mayflower Compact is sometimes seen as crucial in the development of democracy, with its insistence that the people form a "body politic" to pass laws by which all would abide. When we declared our independence from Great Britain, we became more democratic. But our Founding Fathers, those who drew up our Constitution, were, quite frankly, not very democratic. They were a bunch of wealthy, conservative, white men. (That is not bad-mouthing them. Many of them were brilliant, the best generation of minds in American political history, and they created a document that has lasted over 200 years, a remarkable achievement in human history.) It is reported that Alexander Hamilton said once in a conversation when "the people" were mentioned, "The people! The people is a great beast!" Not what most of us would consider a very democratic attitude! So the Founding Fathers created a government well-designed to preserve stability and the status quo, including control by conservative, wealthy, white men like themselves. It's worked really well, hasn't it?!

The point is that "We, the People" have had to work over the centuries to make our system a more democratic one. We insisted that the Bill of Rights (the first ten amendments) be added, and over the years we have insisted on amendments abolishing slavery, giving women the right to vote, giving us the right to elect our own U. S. Senators, lowering the voting age to 18. People's activism has not been limited to Constitutional amendments; many of us participated in the movement for civil rights for all Americans and the movement to end the war in Vietnam, for example. (Parenthetically, surely the next amendment to make our Constitution more democratic should be one abolishing the Electoral College and allowing "We, the People" to actually elect our own President, so that the popular vote cannot be offset by the electoral vote—or, even worse, by the Supreme Court!)

My favorite historian is Howard Zinn, best known for his million-plus seller, *A People's History of the United States*. Notice the title—a *people's* history of the United States. The ideals of the Declaration of Independence, the founding document of our country, are central to Zinn's work—such ideals as life and liberty and the pursuit of happiness and equality and self-determination that are so self-evident and inherent that no government has the right to take them away. Much of Zinn's version of American history is the story of a continuing effort, still by no means complete, to live up to those ideals in reality.

When I was researching my book on Zinn's life and writings, I found a single sheet of paper amidst the materials in his office unattached to anything else. On it were very few words. At the top, like an intended title for something: "The Biggest Secret." Only one line followed: "That we have power." That seems to be related to a passage from his book, *Declarations of Independence* (!), in which he says that "a fundamental principle of democracy" is that "it is the citizenry, rather than the government, that is the ultimate source of power and the locomotive that pulls the train of government in the direction of equality and justice."

"We, the People," indeed!

Three concluding thoughts:

First, a couple of questions in reference to current events: Is violence likely to be an effective way to introduce a people to democracy? Should we be concerned that our own democratic rights here at home are eroding in the name of "security"? (Think "Patriot Act.")

Second, voting is not enough. It's crucial, but it's not enough. Get out there and work for the causes you believe in. That is democracy at its best.

And finally, democracy—what an appropriate theme for a Unitarian Universalist congregation to focus on for a month! The proud tradition of our "liberal religion" relates closely to many of the movements in our country's past for greater democracy. And our congregations exercise "congregational" polity; that is to say, in a UU church, it is "We, the People" who make the decisions!

☮

A couple of years later, I was asked to write an essay on the theme of justice. Here's that one, from *Simple Gifts* in January, 2006, not quite so long.

☮

Justice. It's a powerful word, isn't it? My dictionary reminds me that it means "the quality of being just [just=guided by truth, reason, justice, and fairness]; righteousness, equitableness, or moral rightness"; also "the moral principle determining just conduct—conforming to this principle, as manifested in conduct."

Justice. A powerful concept indeed! And I would suggest it is close to the heart of both Christianity and our country.

First the latter. When we say those words "with liberty and justice for all" in the Pledge of Allegiance, we know it's not literally true, don't we, that we have not ever quite reached that goal? But what a wonderful concept to base a country on! And it is a major part of the founding document of our country, the Declaration of Independence, which speaks of such ideals as life and liberty and the pursuit of happiness and equality and self-determination that are so self-evident and inherent that no government has the right to take them away.

Our November 2004 monthly theme here at All Souls was "democracy." Clearly, the two—democracy and justice—are not unrelated. My favorite historian, Howard Zinn, best known for his million-plus seller, *A People's History of the United States*, has helped me to understand this, writing that "a fundamental principle of democracy" is that "it is the citizenry, rather than the government, that is the ultimate source of power and the locomotive that pulls the train of government in the direction of equality and justice." So democracy is the method that "We, the People" use to move toward justice!

I have stated that justice is close to the heart of Christianity also. Look at the story of the Good Samaritan. Jesus tells us in that parable of our obligation to take care of our neighbor, and it is clear that our neighbor is anyone who needs our help. In short, he tells us to do justice! In the Old Testament, the same idea shows up repeatedly. My favorite? Amos saying "let justice roll down like waters, and righteousness like an ever-flowing stream." The Rev. Dr. Martin Luther King, Jr., liked to quote that. Will and Ariel Durant, in their massive *The Story of Civilization*, summarized the great philosopher Spinoza's critique of the Bible, then quoted him as saying it is a sufficient creed to believe in "a God . . . who loves justice and charity," and whose proper worship "consists in the practice of justice and love towards one's neighbor." Conclude the Durants: "No other doctrine is necessary."

I recently read Jim Wallis's *God's Politics*. It presents a powerful peace- and justice-based vision of Christianity. Since when, Wallis asks, did Jesus become pro-war and pro-rich?! Instead, Jesus showed a consistent commitment to helping the poor and promoting peace; "Blessed are the Peacemakers," remember? Don't let the "Religious Right" define Christianity.

But maybe you're one of those Unitarian Universalists who is uncomfortable with Christianity? No problem. Two of our seven UU principles focus on justice. The second: "Justice, equity, and compassion in human relations." And the sixth: "The goal of world community with peace, liberty, and justice for all."

In short, feel good—your religion and your country are both committed to justice. In principle. But don't forget that part of the definition about "manifested in conduct." It's our job to bring about justice!

There are those, perhaps even among the readers of this volume, who might find things like democracy and justice strange themes for focal points in the life of a church. Two points: Jesus himself was perhaps more concerned with justice than anything else; and remember that what I'm searching for is "relevant" religion. But also, other, more traditional themes were a part of the church year, including Vision, Creation, God, Evil, Authority, Redemption, and Mercy.

Finally, on this business of themes that hopefully show the relevance of religion, the theme for December, 2006, was peace. I was not involved in any "official" way this time, but I did share some thoughts with my minister, The Rev. Marlin Lavanhar, in an e-mail message. I began by noting that I was writing to him on a Sunday morning (November 12), at a time when I "ought to be in church," but that Carole and I were at our get-away cottage on Lake Spavinaw, which we found "more peaceful" than Tulsa. (The very next year, we sold the Tulsa house and moved to Spavinaw full-time.) I told Marlin that peace was "an issue I care about deeply." I noted that it was especially appropriate that peace be our theme for December, when we celebrate the birthday of Jesus, known among other things as "The Prince of Peace." Further thoughts included these:

> Peace . . . do we mean the absence of war between countries? Or do we mean INNER peace? Maybe the latter is necessary to help lead to the former? But we can't WAIT for everybody to achieve inner peace, can we? We need peace ACTIVISM as well. I spoke to the Tulsa Peace Fellowship a few months back. A young man showed up who was into meditation/inner peace; he had seen the word "Peace" in the title of the program, and just dropped in. He wanted, I believe, to argue that all we needed to do was each of us work on our own inner peace; hopefully we convinced him that that is not enough!

I noted the close relationship between peace and justice, the theme I had most recently worked on, noted that I wish sometimes I could be a pacifist, but have "never been quite able to get there, rejecting ALL war, maybe in part because as a historian I see certain wars as necessary? Maybe the Civil War had to be fought to end the evil of slavery? Maybe World War II had to be fought to stop the evil of Naziism?" And finally I told Marlin that I had recently seen a woman in Nevada wearing a button that said "Ask me about the Department of Peace." I did so, I told him, "And she reminded me that there is indeed a group devoted to having a cabinet-level position devoted to peace —makes sense to me!"

I have mentioned Rev. Lavanhar a number of times. He is, in my opinion, doing an excellent job of carrying on an important tradition at All Souls. In 2007, when I put together my second collection of what I like to call "alternative views" of Oklahoma history, *Alternative Oklahoma: Contrarian Views of the Sooner State*, I asked him to contribute an essay, essentially dealing with All Souls and the role it has played in Tulsa over the years. He began by noting that Tulsa has sometimes been considered "the buckle of the Bible Belt," but insisted that "at the beginning of the twenty-first century, religion in Tulsa is much more multifaceted and progressive" than that title implies. He proceeded to make the case convincingly that Tulsa has been, in some ways, "a religiously progressive city for decades." As evidence, he pointed out that Tulsa's Council of Churches was the first in the nation to admit Catholics (1965), then Unitarians and Jews (1971), and, after changing its name to Tulsa Metropolitan Ministries, became the first in the nation to admit Muslims (1983). Additionally, he emphasized the way Tulsa's religious communities had come together to accomplish good in the city, including the Day Center for the Homeless, Retired Seniors' Volunteer Program, and Meals on Wheels.

Noting that All Souls has become the largest Unitarian Universalist church in the world, he insisted, I believe accurately, that "There is, in fact, a significant connection between the presence of All Souls in Tulsa and the development of a liberal religious spirit of tolerance and cooperation in the city." All Souls, he wrote, "became a force in the city when it came to responding to social ills." One of the well-known expressions at All Souls, he said, is "Deeds not Creeds." Thus, "The church has long taught that it is not what you *say* you believe, but rather how you act in the world that makes for a moral and religious life. The church and its members have played active roles in the movements for women's rights, civil liberties and civil rights, and women's right to choose regarding reproductive services." As just one concrete example: The Rev. John B. Wolf was involved in the civil rights movement early on, in the 1960s, and Rev. Lavanhar now serves on the board of Tulsa's John Hope Franklin Center for Reconciliation.

Marlin writes this near the end of his essay:

> All Souls is part of what is known as the Free Church tradition, which sees God's work in the world in the unfolding of freedom. Such freedom is recounted in the Jews' exodus from Egypt, the American Revolution, the abolition of slavery in America, and the ending of apartheid in South Africa. God is seen working in the world, in the light of scientific pursuits and discoveries and the freedom of people to have self-determination regarding their national and religious leaders. In such a tradition, freedom of thought and unhindered exploration of religious ideas and truths are the norm. Such a culture allows for powerful and potent discussions to take place and for new ideas to take root. Ministers are given the freedom to preach without the restraints of established doctrine and dogma. Laypersons are not expected to agree with everything the minister says; they are encouraged to think for themselves and to let their conscience be their guide.

For me, that is an excellent description of a relevant religion.

In conclusion, I have no intention here of preaching to you, of trying to convert you to my point of view on religion. I hope it's obvious that I have a deep respect for many different religious traditions (and even for those individuals who choose not to practice any organized religion at all). If you believe, as I stated earlier, that a "good religion" is one which sustains you, fulfills you, and makes you a better person, surely you can see that the very existence of so many different religions—and so many approaches to the same religion—indicates that it takes a variety of approaches to do that for people. I still believe that being a Unitarian Universalist does it for me.

CHAPTER 9

Common Ground Farm and Oklahoma Character

This chapter was originally presented as a paper at the Red Dirt Book Festival, a wonderful celebration of books that is focused each time on an Oklahoma theme. The festival is put on by the Pioneer Library System, and takes place in the fall every odd year in Shawnee. What I attempt here, as will be clear, is a history and interpretation of Common Ground Farm, the intentional community in southeastern Oklahoma where our daughter has lived now for over 30 years. Note that this chapter begins to move the book toward its conclusion by focusing on Oklahoma. I should also note that versions of the essay appeared in both *The Oklahoma Revelator* (Volume I, Number 1, August, 2008), and the *Red Dirt Anthology 2007*.

☮

Introduction

Nestled in the beautiful Kiamichi Mountains of southeastern Oklahoma lies a little piece of Heaven called Common Ground.

Perhaps that sentence makes obvious that this will not be a traditional scholarly paper?

Our daughter, Elizabeth, is one of the owners of Common Ground Farm. My wife, Carole, and I love to go there, have for over a quarter of a century. We love the people, the land, the quiet. But I am a historian, so I promise you I will try to keep my facts straight. Besides, historical objectivity is a myth, don't you think? I learned that from Howard Zinn many years ago.

The best we can do is to be open and honest and up front about our biases, then proceed to write the best history we can write, being true to the sources. That's what I'm going to do here. Consider this a history and interpretation of Common Ground Farm, with an effort to relate it to the theme of the 2007 Red Dirt Book Festival, "Oklahoma Character." My sources, by the way, are the documents that relate to Common Ground's history (somewhat limited, as many were destroyed accidentally some years back), interviews (primarily via e-mail) with most of the residents and former residents, and personal experience/ observation. (By the way, Common Ground is the real name, but I'm not being specific as to location and I'm using only first names of individuals involved to respect their privacy.)

Outstanding Oklahoma writer Rilla Askew wrote this as the opening paragraph of her novel, *The Mercy Seat*:

> There are voices in the earth here, telling truth in old stories. Go down in the hidden places by the waters, listen: you will hear them, buried in the sand and clay. Walk west in the tallgrass prairie; you'll hear whispering in the bluestem. Stand here, on the ragged rim of a mountain in the southeastern corner; you can hear the sound rising on the south wind, sifting in the dust through the crowns of the cedars: stories told in old voices, in the pulse of bloodmemory; sung in the hot earth above the ceaseless thrum of locusts and nightbirds whillowing, beneath the faint rattle of gourd shells. One story they tell is about longing, for this is a place of homesickness. The land has become home now, and so the very core of this land is sorrow. You can hear it longing for the old dream of itself. Like this continent. This country. Oklahoma. The very sound of it is home.[1]

Isn't that beautiful? But you know what, residents of Common Ground can state it almost as eloquently. Max, for example, one of the original four owners, said with obvious passion in his interview that being "restless" was part of the Oklahoma character. "We couldn't have done this in California," he said. "I'm proud to be an Okie; I claim it! I did it in reverse, came from California to here. Maybe I feel this more than others because my grandfather was from here, but to me, there's no place more beautiful; this feels like home!" (Glen, one of the four current owners, once used the expression "reverse Okies.") Max even noted that he doesn't get chiggers, rarely gets ticks, two problems that just about everybody who has been to southeastern Oklahoma in the summer knows about; "it's in the blood," he bragged.

The Basic Story

Max, his brother Don, and their friends Arthur and Dan, first moved to southeastern Oklahoma in 1974. But Common Ground as such did not yet exist. They lived on 80 acres they called "Earthborne," and built a cabin there. It was a while later when they purchased the current 120 acres and incorporated as "Common Ground." Max and Don were native Texans, Arthur from California, and Dan from Washington. In Max's case, the move involved dropping out of college and loading everything in a Volkswagen bus. Some of the men, he says, met their partners/spouses through involvement in the anti-nuclear power movement, specifically the successful effort to stop Public Service Company of Oklahoma's proposed Black Fox plant near Inola, east of Tulsa; others met through other channels in Tulsa, including Neighbor for Neighbor, a coop. All four of the original guys remember what was to emerge as one of the central difficulties of the residents of Common Ground: making a living. At one time or another, they all worked in Tulsa and commuted; eventually, most of them got odd jobs nearby, some working for Weyerhauser planting trees.

The memories of Max's eventual wife, Alice, add an eloquent touch to all this. "It was wonderful to enter such a peaceful, healthy environment that was free from cars and the business of city life," she says. "It was pure bliss to arrive on a dark moonlight night to see our friends gathering in the lantern-lit cabins, cooking and laughing together." But she also remembers the hard work. Life on Common Ground, she says, "was not a breeze, as many outsiders assumed. Actually, I had never worked harder preparing each day's food and keeping up with the list of chores that go with living with no electricity or running water."

Arthur remembers the combination of good times and hard work involved in "living off the land," as well. By the time they acquired Common Ground, two women, Danna (with Don) and Viva (with Dan) had been added to the group. Arthur credits

Max with creating the name Common Ground, and considers it "perfect . . . for all that was to take place on this piece of dirt in the years to come."

Adds Don: "To make a conscious choice, to act on it, to drop out and tune in, was an act of bravery. I always thought that our initial exodus from California was a reverse 'dust-bowl' effect. Okies, like my parents, left Oklahoma in the thirties to heal a hungry belly. We came to Oklahoma to heal our discontented minds. And Oklahoma nurtured us."

The Mission Statement that the owners agreed to reads: "Common Ground is an intentional community comprised of both resident and non-resident members and owners. Through this intentional community, we are committed to working together, to enjoying each other's company, and to sharing and preserving Common Ground Farm." Even that is powerful, I think, but documents that exist further clarifying the group's goals include "Common Ground Philosophy Statement" which bears quoting in full:

> We are a collective group of individuals.
>
> We accept the challenge to show ourselves, our children and the world that people can live together harmoniously, consciously, and happily. To that end, we understand the importance of supporting and trusting each other.
>
> We value each person's input and strive for equality amongst ourselves.
>
> We practice conflict resolution in the group and individually. In doing so, we pledge to take responsibility for resolving conflict, whether that be in meetings or privately with another member.
>
> We respect non-violence.
>
> We are dedicated to reaching group decisions through consensus and understand that struggling together over issues strengthens the group.
>
> We believe we are also gathered together to work toward ending injustice. We encourage individuals to be politically active in the larger community, and align ourselves with the philosophies of environmentalism, feminism, child advocacy, and tolerance of all races and cultures.
>
> We respectfully challenge our own prejudices and ignorance, and hope to always be learning better ways to reach common ground.

Powerful stuff, many of us might say—certainly I do. But also suggestive perhaps of why Common Grounders were initially regarded by many locals as a bunch of hippies who didn't fit in and weren't really welcome, of which more later.

Owners/residents have come and gone over the years, in a pattern too complex to trace in detail here, and there's really no need. Some of those individual stories will emerge as we continue. Suffice it for now to say that there are currently four owners: Arthur, Elizabeth, Glen, and David—notice that only Arthur is left of the original four. Also, only Arthur and Elizabeth are full-time residents of Common Ground.

Max, Alice, Don, Danna, Arthur, Dan, Glen, and Sally entered into a "Partnership Agreement" on January 10, 1979. That document still exists, and while it shows some of the high ideals of the group, is mostly a formal legal document; such principles as common ownership and consensus, however, are present even there.

There's also a more detailed document from 1998 showing that Don and Danna, Max and Alice, and Dan are no longer a part of Common Ground, while Elizabeth, David, and Tom and Susan have been added to the ownership group. This document, entitled "Operating Agreement of Common Ground, L.L.C.," is far more detailed and includes much legal jargon, doubtless necessary, but some of the high ideals can still be found between the lines.

Clearly, events for Common Ground had reached a bit of a crisis stage by June 12, 2002, when Elizabeth and Arthur addressed a message to "All Ground Members." While our "interpersonal relationships are intact," they insist, "Our intentional community relationships are waning and fading." Insisting that there was no "blame," that they respected "the individual choices everyone has made," they also insisted that while "CG has been condensing for some time and the core amount left always seemed enough," that "Non-residents seemed better than none at all," the conclusion was that "Now, with only 2 adult members living here, the core amount is not enough." This document is really a plea for help. Though insisting that Common Ground is still "viable and alive," Arthur and Elizabeth are asking for everyone's assistance in coming up with new ideas.

One result of this crisis was the beginning of a new category of membership known as Common Ground Family, people who participate and contribute but are not actually part of the ownership; at present there are three such people, Lucy, my wife Carole, and myself. And the most recent result, dated November 4, 2005, is a "Five Year Plan." This plan includes five goals; each goal is followed by objectives and "Action Steps." The first goal is "To establish an Outreach Committee;" objectives include "making Common Ground more accessible to children" and the establishment of a newsletter. Goal number two is "To prepare a 5-year budget and fundraising plan." One of the objectives here is to "incorporate as a not-for-profit foundation," which Elizabeth is currently working on. The third goal is "Construction of a covered shelter and bath house with attention to alternative methods." Number four is "To enhance environmental awareness" by cleaning up junk and trash, and performing ecological/environmental awareness projects (one sub-item here is the building of a labyrinth, which is underway). Finally, the fifth goal is "To establish 'simple cabins' in the future for new or existing members."

Common Ground doesn't belong to a food cooperative as it once did; with only two full-time residents, it doesn't seem viable, but also perhaps it is not as necessary with the availability now of such places as Wild Oats, Elizabeth suggested. Common Ground *does* have a membership in Sam's Club. That will surely be surprising to some; it is used, apparently, primarily for the purchase of needed equipment.

As Arthur and Elizabeth concluded in their 2002 appeal for help and new ideas, Common Ground, while "viable and alive," has "changed into a different animal."

The Interviews

I submitted five questions to all current and former owners of Common Ground. Not all of them responded, but most did —enough for certain patterns to emerge, some of which seem relevant for the theme of "Oklahoma Character."

First, I asked "When, how, and why did you become involved in Common Ground? (And, for those of you who are no longer a part of it, when/why/how did you end your relationship?)" Some of those answers have already helped tell the basic story, but others deserve fuller attention here. Says Glen: "The concept as I have come to explain it over the years was, 'that individually a hippie could not afford anything, but collectively a bunch of hippies investing together could afford something.'" He saw the idea as "something that might just work," and concluded, "It obviously did work for me, as I am still involved." Glen also noted that he was "very proud to be involved," even though he does not get to spend much time at Common Ground; he sees it, he says, as "a haven for me to look forward to and enjoy . . . ."

Elizabeth—like Glen, involved with Common Ground since 1979—says it was two things that caused her to move there: she was "attracted first to the people and family of Common Ground. But when I came to the land is when I fell in love with the place."

Don, though he is among those who moved on ("got to pay the bills," he notes), seems near-ecstatic about his connection to Common Ground. "I often replay the times," he notes, ". . . eating beans but living large, and most importantly, helping, sharing, and loving each other and our community. A more enriching experience I cannot imagine." Even though he, and others, have moved on, "our spirits and loves remain bonded, untouched by time or distance. This family, our family, is the living proof that the path we chose was the right one, the path with heart. Our dynamic family evolved from the heart and reaches far beyond our little place in the woods." Don's brother, Max, as we have already seen, though he also left—admittedly for greater comforts, such as running water, for himself and his family—still lives nearby and waxes eloquent about his love of both the land and the people of Common Ground. So does his wife, Alice. She notes that though they live and work in Dallas, they spend as much time as they can at their place just two miles from their friends on Common Ground. Writing in third person, she concludes: "Though they live in Dallas, they are

Okies at heart, because they feel the most at home with the gentle, laidback folks in Oklahoma. They will one day retire . . . there and hopefully share this peaceful place they own with their friends and grandchildren in the years to come."

Tom and Susan are among those who left Common Ground, mostly for financial reasons, but they both have strong, positive memories and feelings. Susan remembers that "the initial groups's disbanding and discord was increasing," but also remembers her love of the land and "more happy memories." Tom says, "The knowledge gained about how to be self-sufficient in living with the world and in the world by gardening, foraging, and sometimes hunting raised my confidence for being able to take care of myself regardless of what the future brings. It helped me be aware of the importance of caring for this wonderful planet and its living things."

David's flowing response to my questions again approaches eloquence. Just a small piece of it here: "Common Ground is as relevant to me today as it was when I first became a part of it. It is a place in the mind as much as a place on the map. It is a place of possibilities and health and imagination. It is spacious and open and accepting. It is a place to dream, to create, to recharge. It is larger than the sum of its parts, and will live on in the hearts of all who have spent time here."

The second question allows us to get closer to the theme of Oklahoma Character—though I hope you will agree that some of what we have covered already is relevant for that theme. The question was, "What does Common Ground MEAN to you? Did being a part of it change your perspective on the world? How do you see the future of Common Ground?" As you see, these questions are not mutually exclusive; they overlap, and so, not surprisingly, the answers do as well. Thus, some individuals have already made significant comments about what Common Ground means to them. But here are a few more. Glen's answer, in a word, is "community." Being a part of it didn't change his perspective, he says, as he was already part of a group of musicians focused on a common goal, so Common Ground was a logical extension of that. The future? His greatest concern is financial: The "biggest gap" in the original plan, he thinks, "was the lack of a common way to generate income for the group," and "To continue into the future, the community has to be able to provide financial support for the community outside of the individual members."

Elizabeth is the eloquent one here. Community is her central word, like Glen's. The land itself would have been enough to make her want to move to Common Ground, she says, but she wouldn't actually have done it without the community. "I came here when 20, and have been here for 28 years now," she says. "So naturally, the land and the community has raised me. . . . I do not do well if I am gone for long periods of time away from the farm. I am spoiled by the lack of air pollution, noise pollution, crime, [and the presence of] green and fresh water, indigenous rare plants, and more rocks than I know what to do with." As for the future, "The land will always be protected," she says. "It will look the way it looks now, change with the weather, but be protected from corporate interests, and sheltered by our deep connection to protecting the earth. As long as I live. After that, ..." She leaves it up in the air that way—which is, of course, the only honest thing to do with the future.

Arthur is more practical. Community and the land are central to his answer here. But he also speaks strongly: "A simple answer to the question, 'what does Common Ground mean to me' would be 'a lot.' I've given it my life, so far." Being a part of the experience has not really changed his perspective, he thinks, but rather "reinforced my belief in the idea that basically most people are good, decent souls and given a chance will come through for one another. Also, the fact that diverse people, with radically different personalities, can come together and learn to work together for the purpose of a common goal." The future? Arthur states it in terms of what he would *like* to see: "For the future, I would like to see a continuance of the commitment we started. People with a commitment to each other, committed to preserving this land."

Don didn't divide his response to my questions, but rather gave one long, flowing answer. The part that seems most relevant here is where he boils the meaning of Common

Ground down to "Love of others, love of the land, and don't be afraid of hard work;" of course, he also adds "or being naked in the garden."

Alice *hopes* that Common Ground "will go on as a legacy to our loved ones in years to come as an example of what is possible when men, women, and children join hands for the good of the earth and support of each other."

Tom in response to this question quotes his daughter Kerra: "It's about Friendship, Family, Love, Trust and Beauty." "That says it all," he concludes, and he insists that though he and his family had to move away, he hopes to be able to spend more time at Common Ground in the future.

Finally, David insists that the "great quantifier of American life—money" was secondary to him and the folks of Common Ground when he joined up. "Enjoying life, music, knowledge, making a difference, being the best at whatever we endeavored to do, being conscious and aware, living a whole and integrated life—these were our shared ideals. We had a perspective that encompassed more than ourselves and our immediate needs, and being close to nature informed our actions, our sense of community."

My third question was "As you think back over your experience with Common Ground, what positives and negatives come to mind? In other words, strengths and weaknesses, or highs and lows . . ." Obviously, some material relevant to this question has already come out. Says Elizabeth, "The most positive aspect, if not downright amazing aspect, is that we have successfully pulled off an intentional community for 30 years in rural, Southeastern Oklahoma. We have done this with consensus decision making the whole way. No law suits, just tears and hard work." Elizabeth considers "community" to be at the heart of it all, the greatest specific positive, with perhaps the greatest weakness being the failure to "start a business specifically for CG," thus leading to what she calls "the exodus," lots of folks feeling like they had to leave. Though they might state it differently, virtually all respondents agreed with this analysis. Arthur—remember, the only other full-time resident left—combines the community and the land into a single "equation." He says he remembers a meeting years ago in which someone said "It's not the place, but the people." "I had to disagree," he continues, "because for me it's very much both. Both the community and the place. You know, Community/ Land. Or, Common Ground." It has brought him great joy, he says, to "see such a beautiful group of people that are so committed to each other also sharing in such a strong commitment to such a beautiful piece of land." Of course, he also remembers as one of the great positives "the parties," especially but not limited to the annual "Spring Fling" with its campfires, food, music, and fellowship. Tom—a different Tom, currently a part-time resident—even made a video a few years back that was essentially a 25-year history of Spring Fling! Arthur sees Spring Fling, however, as not just a party, but also an "annual reaffirmation and testament to what all of us CG members have accomplished and committed to in the past as well as a nod to what lies ahead for the future." Finally, on the financial point, he notes that since finding work proved especially difficult for the women of Common Ground, the group built a pizza parlor in a nearby town which still thrives.

Knowing that what I hoped to do was present my work about Common Ground at the Red Dirt Book Festival, an event I like so much, and knowing that this year's theme was Oklahoma Character, I asked this question: "The theme of the Red Dirt event is 'Oklahoma Character.' What comes to your mind when you think of Oklahoma character, and how, if at all, do you think Common Ground relates?" Glen's answer is a good start. Briefly reviewing Oklahoma history itself, he focuses on hard work, frugality, and dedication to the family—and he believes all three definitely apply to Common Ground. Elizabeth agrees. She talks about southeastern Oklahoma as in some ways a place slow to change and behind many more populated areas, but also as a place where "people will stop and assist you if you are stranded or in trouble no matter what. . . . In Oklahoma, neighbors are neighbors. At Common Ground, we have taken that philosophy and soaked it in an alternative lifestyle. Oklahoma character gone hippie, gone heartful." Arthur, thinking of Oklahoma, thinks of folks being tenacious, even stubborn, optimistic ("You know, if a tornado destroys someone's home, they make a statement like, well I'm just thankful I still have my garden"), and persevering/steadfast. And, he insists, "Obviously, these are all traits that have helped maintain, sustain and nourish Common Ground." When I suggested, in my interview with Max, that the Joad family in John Steinbeck's *The Grapes of Wrath* was *not* portrayed negatively, as some have insisted, but positively, as people who were strong, hard-working, determined, and who had a strong sense of connection to the land and the family, he agreed, and said, "That describes us also."

My final question was simply asking each respondent if it was okay for me to use the name Common Ground and each individual's first name only; all agreed.

The Children of Common Ground

Several of the adult respondents to my questions made significant comments about the children of Common Ground. Said Arthur: "They all mean so much to me. I'm so glad that we touched them with this wonderful perspective of the 'other way' of living." Max said he believed Common Ground, with its "relation to nature," was "wonderful for children." David wondered if the children would cherish their time on Common Ground, "look back on it with fond memories." Max was "confident they will respond positively." David did not need to wonder; Max was right. In some ways, the children of Common Ground express even stronger positive feelings than their parents—we've already seen Kerra's comment about friendship/family/love/trust/beauty. By "Children of Common Ground," let me clarify, I mean those who spent at least some of their childhood there; obviously, in most cases, we have "met" their parents already. Arthur's daughter, Ashley, says that "most of the amazing times I've had in my life were spent there." She doesn't think being a part of the Common Ground community has changed her perspective on the world, "because I've always been a part of it, so I've never had a perspective other than what I do now. However, I probably would have turned out differently if I hadn't been a part of it."

The questions I asked the children (all now adults) were very similar to the ones I asked the adults. I want to let each child of Common Ground speak to all the questions.

Clancey lived on Common Ground for about four years in the 80s, between about his fourth and eighth birthdays. He says he still thinks of the people of Common Ground as an "extended family." Thoughtfully, he adds that he had trouble adjusting when he left (for Dallas) because "I was deeply entrenched in the Common Ground approach to community involvement where everyone was close to one another, much like I think life must have been for humanity before the rise of technology and the proliferation of large cities." He remembers fondly the "incalculable freedoms" being raised on Common Ground, the "idyllic childhood" spent roaming through the woods and streams. He's concerned about the future of Common Ground. Insightfully, he connects the region being economically depressed with Common Ground being such a special place: "If it had a more vibrant economy, it probably would not be as remote and isolated as it is." Clancey came up with a long list of "positives," or strengths, including "family atmosphere, community involvement, diversity in thinking, learning to go against the grain, environmental responsibility (before it was cool), ability to question and reason, complete freedom of expression, breaking down of barriers, be it age, sex, color, sexual orientation, religious beliefs, political beliefs, economic status." His list of "negatives," or weaknesses, is shorter, but significant: "the region, which has poor economic development, inadequate educational resources, and proliferation of drug manufacturing and use." On Oklahoma character, Clancey says he's afraid the average American views Oklahomans as "backwards" and "hillbillies," but his own image is quite different: "everyday people who have understated personalities and carry with them an immense sense of kindness and friendliness towards others, even complete strangers. This, I think, is the true 'Okie.' The true 'laid back' and 'down home' personality resides in rural Oklahoma."

Skye lived on Common Ground for some thirteen years. He still goes back as often as possible, and remembers fondly that he "spent every summer standing in the waters of the swimming hole all day fishing and hunting for crawdads." Common Ground, he believes, "had more of an impact on my life than any other source." "I learned about neighbors and family," he says, "and that sometimes whether technically or not they are the same." He feels so strongly about all this that he hopes "to become more of a participating member [of Common Ground] in the near future." Responding to the question about positives and negatives, Skye started with this sentence: "I will first start with THE negative since there is really only one and then proceed with the positives, which are never ending until I get tired of typing." His only negative, by now not surprisingly, was "limited financial avenues." His list of positives included safety, beautiful landscapes, and the "positive and supportive people" helping each other all the time. Skye's thoughtful conclusion bears quoting in full: "Common Ground is people living off the land using harmony instead of force to benefit from the land. That is the essence of the rural Oklahoma way; self-sufficient practices along with ideals and hard work to achieve success. The freedom to live how we choose and practice what we believe is not only the Oklahoma way, but the basic structure around which our nation was built. Common Ground embraces those things."

Clancey's brother Colton says that Common Ground has been a part of his life as long as he can remember, and his experience there helped to make him who he is today. He can't think of a single "low," and his comment about Common Ground *in re* Oklahoma character is: "When I think of Oklahoma Character I think of the Native Americans and their love/affinity for Mother Earth. I can say that most who have experience and take part in the goings on at Common Ground certainly share this same love and concern for nature."

Bill remembers being in the third grade when Common Ground began, and though he moved away with his mother some years later, he insists he never ended his relationship with Common Ground—"I have always felt as much part of the community/family as I did in the days I ran around barefoot all over the property." His positives include the land, the family/

community, and his negatives being "seen as weird hippies at first by the locals" and "the realities of finances and working." Thinking of Oklahoma character, Bill says as he travels around the country, when he talks about Oklahoma, "people typically talk about two things: One is that a lot of folks have family in Oklahoma, and two, they speak highly of them as kind/good people." Common Ground, he thinks, fits right in.

Autumn's response is long, flowing, sometimes beautiful and moving. She remembers some parts of being a small child at Common Ground as being a little scary, "like going camping and never coming home," but also "exciting." Part of the legacy of the experience is that she still tries to live close to nature. At about ten or twelve years old, she remembers that she "began to realize that I was enjoying my summers in Oklahoma more than I was liking my life in New York City [where she was living with her father and going to school]," so she moved back to Oklahoma to start seventh grade. After a period of adjustment, involving among other things family difficulties, "I began to really find my groove. For the first time in my life I was happy where I was." She especially loved "the huge extended family," but also swimming, walking in the woods, etc. Autumn is moving in talking about the *meaning* of Common Ground for her. "Common Ground has always been a place of peace for me," she says. "In later years as I've had problems with anxiety and other things I have been taught tools by professionals in which they tell you to go somewhere in your mind, somewhere you love, and picture yourself walking there and the things you see . . . And the beauty and peacefulness of Common Ground never fails to work!" But Common Ground is not just the place, it's also the people: "Common Ground the people mean more than anything in the world to me and not next to my family because they are my family." Trying to think of negatives, Autumn mentions, like almost everyone, that the "lack of resources . . . made it almost impossible to make a living." But she also mentions some "personality clashes and differences and blow ups and tears," and is the only one to suggest that the overwhelmingly positive nature of her Common Ground experience can be seen in one way as a negative. "I went to college and out in the world thinking that basically deep down everyone loves each other and will be there for you if you need them and will hold your confidences and was on your side no matter what and you could do anything with your life and there were no prejudices and no violence and no mean people and so on and so on. It was a rude awakening over a few years to realize that most of that is not the case in the real world." Finally, her brief comment on Oklahoma character: "When I think of Oklahoma character, I think of good, down-home, honest, simple (not in a bad way) people that are about working hard and playing hard. And in a character way I think no differently of the people on Common Ground." Which, I think, provides an excellent transition into . . .

Conclusion: Common Ground Farm and Oklahoma Character (or, as the Red Dirt Book Festival program put it, "Oklahoma Values in an Intentional Community")

As I look back over what I have written, and specifically the comments of the residents and former residents of Common Ground, I find so much about Oklahoma character—and not just in their responses to the specific question about Oklahoma character, but in all their responses. Certain traits recur over and over again, including: love of and connection to the land (or, as some stated it, being "close to nature"), the importance of family (often defined more broadly than just kin), community, hard work (the constant challenge of how to make a living), and hard *play* (Spring Fling is just the most commonly mentioned example of this at Common Ground). Allow me to simply *list* some of the traits that showed up: bravery, restlessness, cooperation, optimism, perseverance, innovation, creativity, resourcefulness, self-reliance, being "gentle, laid-back," frugality, tenaciousness.... It goes on and on. I am aware, of course, that some of those are redundant, different ways of saying the same thing. I am also aware that some of them seem contradictory. And certainly some of them can cut both ways, so to speak. Have you ever thought of that? Compromise, for example, can be seen as a positive, a way of making things work—at Common Ground, one *very* interesting example is the principle of consensus that has always been used to make decisions. But compromise can also be seen as a negative, as in compromising your principles—at Common Ground, some would see the evolution from gardening to coop to buying from local markets and membership in Sam's Club as an example. But I keep thinking of the fictional Joads, a comparison already made above. One Common Ground member wrote that "you have to learn to get along and work things out," and followed that by saying that "There's not much room for the rugged, individualistic American attitude of independent, 'I'll do what I want to' type of thinking." But aren't *both* those approaches a part of American character, Oklahoma character, human nature?

Look back a few paragraphs at Skye's comment about "the essence of the rural Oklahoma way." *Are* the character traits mentioned repeatedly by Common Grounders distinctly rural? Perhaps. In part. But in my own experience in Oklahoma, I find many of those values in small towns as well—and even among some folks in the larger cities. *And,* I would argue, such values are still *valuable* today! Rachel Jackson, of Red Flag Press, has written:

> Oklahoma is a state founded on the values, concerns and needs of rural people. Despite the technological and urban landscape of today's society, rural Oklahomans have valuable wisdom to offer in the public discussion of social improvement. This wisdom, about what is good and what is bad in Oklahoma, often goes unheard in today's metropolitan political climate. Any solutions to problems currently faced in Oklahoma found in agrarian culture and rural traditions can get lost as a result.[2]

But the best of those traditions must *not* be lost; if that happens, Oklahoma will no longer be fully Oklahoma! Even Mike Jones, Associate Editor for the *Tulsa World*, while strongly calling for dropping the word "Okie"—"Stop it!" he writes; "You can call me about anything you care to. Just don't call me Okie."—acknowledges that "Modern usage suggests that the term Okie has become a symbol of pride for Oklahomans, like Yankee or Hoosier or Tex."[3]

Back, for a moment, to the Joads. Fred R. Harris wrote of them in the foreword of my new book, *Alternative Oklahoma*: "*The Grapes of Wrath* is about good, hard-working, sturdy people trying their best to keep body and soul together in hard-scrabble times and conditions over which they had so little control." And to a certain extent, though in different times, isn't that what the story of Common Ground is about also? I wrote, in my proposal for the Red Dirt festival, that "The Joads may have been ignorant, but they were NOT stupid/worthless, but rather strong, determined, survivors, with a strong sense of connection to family and to the land." (I visualize the scene from the movie version in which Grandpa holds a handful of dirt and lets it sift out through his fingers saying "It's my dirt; it ain't no good, but it's mine!" Of course, part of the irony there is that it was *not* his dirt, since he was a sharecropper.) And then I wrote: "Though the members of Common Ground were shunned and considered suspect by the locals when they began their enterprise over 25 years ago, they have now worked their way into the community; I believe that is because they share some of those Oklahoma values! Even their common ownership of the land is related to the thinking of the original Oklahomans, Native American tribes!"

Rilla Askew contributed an essay to a recent volume from the University of Oklahoma Press entitled *Voices from the Heartland*. Appearing in the section of the book on "Sooner Spirit," she called her essay "Most American." She noted that after the Oklahoma City bombing it became common for people to refer to Oklahoma as "America's Heartland." But Askew writes that in her view, "they got the idea right but the anatomy wrong. This state that has long been a cipher and mystery and, like an illegitimate child, unclaimed by any region, is not the heartland; it is the viscera, the underbelly, the very gut of the nation."[4] Is it getting too carried away to suggest that Common Ground is somewhere close to the gut of Oklahoma? One objection some might make to that suggestion is that the political views of Common Grounders tend to be left-leaning. But those objections, I suggest, would be likely to come from those unfamiliar with our state's long and proud progressive traditions. I like to refer to people like Elizabeth (of Common Ground), Rachel Jackson, Woody Guthrie—and, dare I include myself?—as "radical Okie patriots" (or "matriots," perhaps, in the case of the women). To be in touch with our radical roots is also to have a sense of place, and a sense of pride in Oklahoma. During the Centennial year, while I always tried to understand and respect the desires of many of our Native American citizens to avoid celebrating, there are some things in our past I do celebrate. I celebrate Oklahoma populism, progressivism, socialism, civil rights pioneers, anti-war activists, advocates for women's equality, green activists. And I celebrate Common Ground Farm.

John Wooley, in his recent book, *From Blue Devils to Red Dirt: The Colors of Oklahoma Music*, suggested that "Music seems to be a part of the people's lives there [in Oklahoma], more so than in other states." Actually, he quotes Capitol Records Nashville executive Buzz Stone saying that. Certainly music is a vital part of Common Ground Farm, especially the annual Spring Fling, when one of the rituals is music around the campfires *and* in the shed (with full amplification!). Wooley also suggests that the character of the state is related to the character of the music. "Oklahoma's music is different, at least in part, because of the spirit of brotherhood and the character of the people—a statewide character at least partly forged by the hardships and challenges of the Great Depression of the late '20s and '30s, exacerbated in Oklahoma's case by the Dust Bowl. In order for people to survive, they—at least many of them—learned that they had to take care of one another, to share what they had, to understand that everyone was in it together, and if something happened to one, it could happen to all of them. The idea is that a sense of personal social consciousness is carried like a cultural memory in the minds and hearts of Oklahoma's musical artists." Wooley even relates this to radical politics, specifically to the anti-nuclear power movement—which, remember, brought many of Common Ground's original residents together. He quotes John Cooper, of the popular Oklahoma band the Red Dirt Rangers, saying that "[Bob] Childers [sometimes referred to as the "godfather" of Red Dirt music] even went to Washington during a [1979] rally and sang on the Capitol steps in front of 50,000 people. It was a huge national protest, and there was a big contingent from Stillwater and the Tulsa area because of Black Fox. That was a real galvanizing time for Red Dirt, because it brought a lot of people from the anti-nuke movement into the music." Wooley concludes that "Bob Wills' escapism and Woody Guthrie's social conscience, mixed into the musical forms of the day, became the philosophical and spiritual influences on the developing Red Dirt style."[5] Escapism and social conscience—both are heard on Common Ground.

Harry Menig wrote of Okemah, Woody Guthrie's home town, that it was "in a sense, Woody Guthrie's foster parent. From its people he learned music, charity, hatred, violence, but most of all, a sense of 'getting along'—a need for self-survival through cooperation."[6]   Common Ground is still "getting along."

Max, in his interview, referred to Elizabeth as the "spirit" of Common Ground and Arthur as the "hard worker." Clearly, both are needed. And perhaps, as long as both are present—remember, they are the only two full-time residents of Common Ground left—Common Ground will survive, and we will still be able to say:

Nestled in the beautiful Kiamichi Mountains of southeastern Oklahoma lies a little piece of Heaven called Common Ground.

---

1 Rilla Askew, *The Mercy Seat* (New York: Viking Penguin, 1997), p. 1.

2 Rachel Jackson, flyer announcing Red Flag Press's "Statewide Rural Essay Contest–Oklahoma: The Good, The Bad, and The Better." For more information, visit www.redflagpress.com.

3 Mike Jones, "Smile when you say that, pardner–Better yet, just don't say it at all," *Tulsa World*, December 30, 2007.

4 Rilla Askew, "Most American," in Carolyn Anne Taylor, Emily Dial-Driver, Carole Burrage, and Sally Emmons-Featherston, Eds., *Voices from the Heartland* (Norman: University of Oklahoma Press, 2007), p. 5.

5 John Wooley, *From Blue Devils to Red Dirt: The Colors of Oklahoma Music* (Tulsa: Hawk Publishing Group, 2006), pp. 131, 137, and 139-40.

6 Harry Menig, "Woody Guthrie: The Oklahoma Years, 1912-1929," in Davis D. Joyce, Ed., *"An Oklahoma I Had Never Seen Before:" Alternative Views of Oklahoma History* (Norman: University of Oklahoma Press, 1994), p. 163.

CHAPTER 10

Progressive Past / Conservative Present
Oklahoma's Political History / Mystery

This chapter obviously continues the Oklahoma focus of the previous one; it also was originally presented at the Red Dirt Book Festival, specifically the 2005 event for which the theme was "Mysterious Oklahoma." People so often have asked me, "How did Oklahoma move from the progressive past you talk about so much to the incredibly conservative place it is today?" The essay that follows represents my brief attempt to answer that question. It also comes full circle back to the idea of the personal/historical, including teaching history in a relevant manner that might contribute to a better present—and future. Before I get to it, though, I have a lot more to say.

I said some of it in a letter of March 5, 2010, to both of Oklahoma's United States Senators, Tom Coburn and James Inhofe. This is part of what I wrote:

☮

This is probably unusual, but I'm sending the same letter to both of you, as I want to say essentially the same things to both of you; when something applies to just one of you, I'm confident you'll be able to figure it out.

The basic thing is this: I am, in many ways, a proud Oklahoman. . . . I am well aware that Oklahoma is a "red state" in today's political terminology, but I'm also well aware, as a historian, that our state has proud progressive/left/liberal/ radical elements in both our past and our present. I am aware that history tends to go in cycles, so I hope we'll be cycling back to some of those roots, and that the two of you can move on to new careers. I'm not just waiting for that cycle to occur, but rather working to make it happen, thus this letter.

Just a few specific thoughts:

The Family: It's hard to find out many details about it, which is part of the problem, since you were elected by the people of Oklahoma to a PUBLIC office. But everything I know tells me it is an insult to Christianity to say it has anything to do with Christianity. Friendly reminder: Jesus talked about peace (blessed are the peacemakers, remember?), helping the poor and hungry, and love for ALL people, even your enemies. (My life-long devout Southern Baptist Mother, who died at 94 just over a year ago, was very angry the last few years of her life at those on the so-called "religious right" who claimed to be speaking for Christianity. We talked about how they seemed to be trying to make Jesus sound pro-rich, pro-war, filled with hate for those who are different. I will never forget the way she looked at me and said in a weak voice but with strong conviction, "Well, that's certainly not the Jesus I know!")

Obstructionism: Vote your conscience, but don't try to find tricks to keep the majority will from prevailing.

Hypocrisy: If you truly think the economic stimulus was a bad thing, say so, but say so consistently; don't say so in Washington and then come home to Oklahoma and act like you think it's a great thing (and that you deserve credit for it).

Climate change: It's my understanding that over 90% of the scientists who are qualified to have an expert opinion on the matter say that global warming is indeed occurring, and that human activity is part of the cause . . .

Health care reform: I have had the experience of living briefly in England and more extensively in Hungary. Based on that experience, I can say confidently: "Socialized medicine" is not a bad thing! People's basic health care needs are taken care of. Our health care system today is perhaps the highest QUALITY in the world. But it falls way short in terms of accessibility, and it is far too costly, and in a way which clearly favors insurance companies and pharmaceutical companies. Why can't we work together on ways to improve it?!

All this, by the way, has nothing to do with political party. I'm registered as a Democrat, but am not too happy with many of them these days either. And as a historian, I know that, as a Republican, you can lay claim to, in my opinion, the greatest man ever to live in the White House. Here's a quote from him that I only recently discovered and love: "Labor is prior to and independent of capital. Capital is only the fruit of labor, and could never have existed if labor had not first existed. Labor is the superior of capital, and deserves much the higher consideration." Do you know those words? They are from Abraham Lincoln!

I have a lot of respect for *The Oklahoma Observer* . . . please . . . read the passionate guest piece by Edwin E. Vineyard in the January 25 issue, "Oh, For A Return To Civil Discourse." Indeed! Civil discourse with those with whom you differ—what a concept! Difficult to do today. I hope I am not being guilty of being uncivil in this letter. That is not my intent. I believe strongly in communicating with those with whom I differ, learning from them, etc. I'd like more evidence of that from the two of you.

Thanks for your attention, have a nice life, both of you.

☮

I received a perfunctory, totally non-committal response from Senator Inhofe, no response at all from Senator Coburn.

You see, I am aware that I am out of touch with the views of the majority of folks who vote in Oklahoma these days. But I would argue that they in turn are out of touch with the left/liberal/progressive/radical aspects of our state's history. And part of my mission is to keep reminding people of those parts of our past, in the hope that we might get back to them.

As I wrote in the preface to my 1994 book, *"An Oklahoma I Had Never Seen Before:" Alternative Views of Oklahoma History*:

> I love Oklahoma. I love its land, its people. I love its history. But, just as I always thought the bumper sticker slogan "America: Love It or Leave It" was silly, narrow-minded, and inappropriate —I always liked "America: Change It or Lose It" better—I react

> negatively to those who react predictably negatively to every
> criticism of Oklahoma. Love it or leave it? No. Some of us love
> it enough to stay and try to change it—America *and* Oklahoma.

I went on to quote one of the famous passages from Howard
Zinn's *A People's History of the United States* in which he insisted that
taking sides in history is inevitable, and that he preferred to tell
the story of America from the point of view of the common
people, the underdog, the outsider, the radical. Then I attempted
a parallel paragraph about Oklahoma history, which appears in
the essay below. I would not argue, of course, that this is the only
approach, to history in general or to Oklahoma history in
particular, but that it is an approach, and one that is much
needed, especially in today's dominant climate of opinion.

Back, for a moment, to my love of Oklahoma. Carole and I
were on a cruise a couple of years ago. We were assigned to a
table with a guy named James from Illinois who was incredibly
ignorant of Oklahoma and its history, especially the kind of
history I'm talking about, but who was, of course, as those who
are ignorant of the facts frequently are, more than willing to
express strong opinions. He actually referred to Oklahoma as a
"retard state." Never mind the inappropriateness of the word
"retard"—I threw a fit! I lost control. I remember Carole on one
side and our good friend Anthony on the other both reaching
over to touch me and try to calm me down. I don't even know
what all I said. I just know that my love of Oklahoma came
through loud and clear.

When I retired a few years ago, I remember thinking
momentarily that someplace like northern Minnesota might be
nice. But that was strictly because I have serious problems with
Oklahoma's heat and humidity every summer. The fact is, Carole
and I never seriously considered moving anywhere else. My
favorite syllable of the state's name is the third one—Oklahoma
is my home.

A guy named Preston Enright in Denver, Colorado, created a
"Listmania!" list at Amazon.com a couple of years ago called
"Progressive Oklahoma." That may seem like an oxymoron to
someone like James, but it isn't—there were forty items on
Enright's list, including books and music albums, and I'm proud
to say that both my collections of alternative views of Oklahoma

history were among them, along with Danney Goble's outstanding book, *Progressive Oklahoma: The Making of a New Kind of State.*

My friend Charles Angeletti, also from Denver and mentioned several times already in these pages, made a comment a couple of years ago in a letter about "progressive Oklahoma" being just a "historical term/era." Charles and I, by the way, while fundamentally in agreement, seem to like to argue with each other. That comment of his set me off, so I wrote the following in my next letter to him:

> Your comment about "Progressive Oklahoma" . . . really concerns me. WAS "progressive Oklahoma" a "historical term/ era"? Yes. Is that all there is to it? Absolutely not! Some of us in this state are proudly left wing, and think it is important to say so and to live it out as best we can. And part of that, for me, is being aware of our "radical" roots (try Populism, Progressivism, Socialism for starters—"radical" just means of or pertaining to roots or origin, after all, and there's lots of those ideas in the air at the time of our origin as a state), but also realizing that radical/left/progressive/whatever folks and movements have been present throughout our history. That is, after all, what I was trying to show in my two books, with things like progressive religious folks putting their faith to work for peace/justice/etc., civil rights pioneers, successful movements for women's issues such as domestic violence and reproductive choice, gay rights, Woody Guthrie, stopping nuclear power, OKLAHOMA Vietnam Veterans Against the War, and Roxanne Dunbar-Ortiz on growing up Okie—and radical!

It occurs to me that my approach to Oklahoma history has long been a bit outside the mainstream. Among the mildewed clippings I've kept, I find an article from the *Tulsa Tribune* of May 21, 1981, under the headline "History with a difference," about my excitement at teaching Oklahoma history for the first time. The very first quote Ron Wolfe, the author of the piece, used from me was "Too much history is just a public relations job—an attempt to tell what a pretty history the state has." I suggested that we would be taking an "open, questioning, critical kind of stance about history—one that suggests too much white-washing has been going on." My first example was Oklahoma's treatment of minorities, especially African Americans and Native Americans. "You don't have to know much about state history to know those groups really have had it bad," and gave the Tulsa

Race Riot and the Trail of Tears as my two primary examples. I complained also that most of the Oklahoma history textbooks I had seen to that date "don't even mention Woody Guthrie," and insisted that it was because Woody was a radical in many ways, and that "Most people who write Oklahoma history are not of that persuasion, so they don't give it the attention it deserves." The article reminded me that I leaned heavily on guest speakers for my first experience teaching Oklahoma history, including Guy Logsdon to sing Woody Guthrie songs and Danney Goble to talk about his book, new at the time, *Progressive Oklahoma: The Making of a New Kind of State.*

If I've long been outside the mainstream in my approach to Oklahoma history, it's not at all surprising that I'm outside the mainstream of Oklahoma politics, which I have already acknowledged. Indeed, I find another, even older clipping from the *Norman Transcript* that suggests that's been the case for an even longer time. It's dated October 18, 1964, and the headline reads "OU President Criticizes Political Advertisement." I was old enough to vote for the first time in 1964, and I had just signed an ad, along with over 200 other OU faculty, staff, and graduate students, endorsing Democrat Fred R. Harris in his campaign against famous OU football coach Bud Wilkinson. Obviously, in Oklahoma, where OU football is such a big deal, that ad was bound to be controversial. It had been headlined "OU faculty and staff strongly support Fred R. Harris for U. S. Senate." Part of President George L. Cross's complaint was that the headline gave the impression there was some sort of official endorsement of Harris by OU. But the ad did carry, though admittedly in much smaller print than the headline, the information that those of us who signed the ad had paid for it ourselves, and that the university did not endorse candidates for public office. But wait, did I say this episode shows that I have been outside the mainstream of Oklahoma politics for a long time? Fred Harris won that election, remember?! And went on to win his next one, and to represent Oklahomans like myself well for some eight years, including his increasingly anti-Vietnam War views, and to become Democratic National Chair, and to serve on the important Koerner Commission investigating racial disturbances in American cities, and to mount a serious populist-oriented campaign for the Democratic Presidential nomination. So there is hope! (I was honored when Harris agreed to write a foreword for my *Alternative Oklahoma* book a few years ago.)

When I'm working on a book idea, everything that comes up seems to relate. (Though much of it, I find later, actually doesn't —I've used quite a few clippings here, but there are even more that I have not used.) Certainly the presidential election of 2008 related in a very powerful way to my approach to Oklahoma history. Rilla Askew, deserving member of the Oklahoma Writers Hall of Fame, reminded me in the *Tulsa World* of December 20, 2009, that "Paradox and dichotomy dominate our character" in Oklahoma. She notes, as one small but interesting example, that an unidentified Tulsa woman suggested that "men in Oklahoma think they live in the West, and women in Oklahoma think they live in the South." Very thoughtful. But allow me to suggest that many women *and* men in Oklahoma think they live in the South! And that the results of the presidential election of 2008 help to illustrate that fact. That's especially true in the southeastern quadrant of the state, long known as "Little Dixie." But the fact is, the Republican ticket of John McCain and Sarah Palin carried all 77 of Oklahoma's counties, the only state in the union in which that was the case. Does that result have something to do with the fact that Barack Obama is African American? Of course it does. My son Kirk was just the first of many to suggest that to me.

That election set off a firestorm of letters to the editor in state newspapers, among other things. Several in the *Tulsa World* caught my attention enough that I held onto them. Many of them, not surprisingly, reflected the way Oklahoma had voted. One writer, on November 28, responded to earlier suggestions that Oklahoma had shown itself to be "out of step with the rest of the nation" by saying "Oklahoma stuck to its principles and values rather than throwing them away for the sake of change." Among those "issues at the core of Oklahoma's values" he listed anti-gay rights, anti-choice, and pro-school prayer. Another, on December 1, insisted that "When the dust settles, and history is written, it will show that Oklahoma was the only state in all 50 states that voted correctly in this presidential election." "I am proud to be an Okie," concluded this writer.

But occasionally, of course, the other point of view showed up, as in one letter of November 23. This person was "elated with the outcome of the presidential election," but "dismayed and stunned" that Oklahoma had shown its "unenlightened and retrogressive nature" by voting the way it did. This other point of view showed up more frequently, of course, in the pages of Oklahoma's long-time independent journalistic voice, *The Oklahoma Observer*. Frosty Troy himself, the founder of the *Observer*, wrote a front-page piece on "The Politics of Race" that celebrated Barack Obama's nomination, something Troy said he had never dreamed he would see, and talked about how far he had had to come to rise above his racist background in "Little Dixie." Hailey Branson, a journalism student at the University of Oklahoma, wrote an excellent and disturbing piece in the December 10/25 issue entitled "No Future In A State So Full of Hate?" She concluded, "If things do not change here, I cannot see myself staying. And that breaks my heart." The person who wrote the piece in the November 23 *World* had ended by saying "I doubt I will ever see Oklahoma voters be progressive and want change." But I say to both that writer and Hailey: Don't give up! History goes in cycles. Oklahoma was a progressive state once, and it can be again. But it cannot be expected to happen automatically— rather, people have to work to make it happen.

Finally, in the pages of the *Observer*, former Governor David Walters fumed about the way the state had voted, in a piece under the headline "Extreme Oklahoma: State Lumped In With Hayseeds, Appalachia." And in that same issue, November 25, another letter writer reminded readers that being called a liberal is not a bad thing, because it means "open-minded, tolerant of divergent opinions, and exceedingly generous. And Jesus Christ was a liberal and a community organizer like Obama."

Just one more thing before getting to the essay that is supposed to constitute this chapter! After Barack Obama's victory, the Presidential Inaugural Committee announced an essay contest that would give ten winners the chance to make an all-expenses-paid trip to his inauguration. All you had to do was answer the question: "What does this inaugural mean to you?" I couldn't resist. This is what I wrote:

☮

When I participated in civil rights demonstrations as a graduate student working on my Ph.D. in history at the University of Oklahoma in the 60s, I don't think it ever occurred to me that I might live to see the first African American President of the United States—I guess I thought it was just about everybody being treated equally. And it occurs to me that, in a sense, that is what it's about....and now Barack Obama is set to become our President in a few days!

When I try to think what this inauguration means to me, it's difficult to sort out the personal from the professional. Personally, my wife and I made small contributions to the Obama campaign a couple of times, something we've rarely done, and we find it makes us feel more a part of this wonderful historical process. Also on the personal level, we were on a cruise to Hawaii this fall. Frequently, I wore my Obama button. I guess most people didn't like it and stayed silent. Three incidents stand out among those who did respond positively. An older gentleman said quietly to me on a crowded elevator, "Nice button!" I struck up a conversation with a middle-aged couple from Arkansas. I knew they were from Arkansas because the man was wearing a t-shirt from Arkansas State University, and I have a nephew who attended there, and I was born and raised in Arkansas myself. As we had a friendly conversation, I noticed the woman was wearing a button that said "Yellow Dog Democrat." So I felt free to say, "I'll bet you like my button." Her reply was, "Oh, yes!" My favorite: A young man from Thailand was my waiter one morning as I had a cup of coffee alone. I noticed him looking around rather strangely, then realized he was making sure no one else was within range as he began to chant, "O-ba-ma, O-ba-ma!"

Actually, I don't separate out the personal from the professional anymore. I learned a long time ago from Howard Zinn, the famous activist and people's historian, that we can't, really, and shouldn't try. (I wrote a book about his life and writings a few years back.) So my professional response to

Obama's success is something I also feel strongly about personally. I'll focus on two things: Abraham Lincoln, and Oklahoma politics and history.

I don't think much in terms of heroes and heroines in U. S. history. And when I do, they're rarely Presidents/kings/queens/generals/the rich. Rather, they're usually those who worked for change, such as abolishing slavery, granting women equal rights, stopping various unjust wars. But Abraham Lincoln is indeed a hero of mine. As I list the accomplishments of his Presidential administration, I think of only two: our country was saved, and the evil of human slavery was removed. Not bad! And Obama announced his candidacy in the same spot Lincoln did! And he's going to place his hand on the same Bible Lincoln did! Historical indeed! And for me, incredibly exciting.

About Oklahoma: I might as well admit it up front: We were the reddest of the red states in the Presidential election—all 77 counties went for McCain. But about one third of us felt strongly that Obama was the way to go. And as a historian, I have long liked to remind people that there was a time in Oklahoma history when, if you called us a red state, you might be referring to our beautiful red dirt, or the "red" Native American people who either lived here or were forced to come here, or even, most surprising of all to many, you might be referring to the fact that we had more "reds" per capita than any other state in the union! Which is to say that Oklahoma had the strongest Socialist party in the country on the eve of World War I. But the broader point is that Oklahoma has strong progressive or left or liberal or radical strands in its past. Populism, Progressivism, Socialism, Woody Guthrie, civil rights pioneers, advocates for women's equality, for peace, for the environment—Oklahoma has had them all. Obviously, we've gotten more than a bit out of touch with our own progressive past! Some of us just see that as a challenge. History, it's been said many times, is cyclical. I agree. But we can't just sit back and wait for it to recycle. Rather, we the people must work to make it recycle! Some of us see constantly reminding people of our state's progressive past as one way of creating a more progressive present—and future. (I've published two books which are essentially collections of essays taking this approach to Oklahoma history.) But some of us also see political organizing as part of the answer. And by the way, on a not unrelated note, I just learned recently that if you trace Barack Obama's family tree back far enough, you'll find Oklahoma roots there!

So I've never been to a Presidential inaugural. It occurs to me that I've never really felt an intense desire to go to one. But this time....! I'm a retired history professor. This will probably be my last chance. And it's the one I'm most excited about in my lifetime! My wife, Carole, shares this feeling. We're realistic—we know the incredible challenges President Obama faces, starting with Iraq and the economy.

Did I just say "President Obama"?! Pardon me for reverting back to the 60s to express my feelings about that: "Wow, man . . . far out!"

Thanks for your consideration.

☮

I didn't win the trip. But I stand proudly by what I said, and hope that it reflects the "personal/historical" theme of this book, and just a bit of my approach to Oklahoma history. You see, when I did my two Oklahoma history books (*"An Oklahoma I Had Never Seen Before"* and *Alternative Oklahoma*), it was not just to please some dean or to get a raise or a promotion, but rather because I care deeply about the state, and my alternative approach to its history is deeply personal.

At last, the essay from the *Red Dirt Anthology 2005* that gives this chapter its title appears below.

☮

I was not present at the Red Dirt Book Festival 2003, but I heard rave reviews from several people who were. So when the call went out for 2005, I quickly responded with a proposal for a paper carrying the above title [Progressive Past/Conservative Present: Oklahoma's Political History/Mystery]. My proposal was worked into a panel on Oklahoma political history. Other participants were to be Roxanne Dunbar-Ortiz and William Welge; sadly, Welge was unable to attend.

Here is the text of my proposal:

David R. Morgan of the University of Oklahoma recently wrote in *The Oklahoma Observer,* "We sometimes forget how radical Oklahoma's political past has been." Indeed we do! The basic reason seems to be that Oklahoma's political/social/cultural conservatism today does not match up very well with the progressive/radical elements of our past. But I have made it a special project, in my book *"An Oklahoma I Had Never Seen Before:" Alternative Views of Oklahoma History* (and a follow-up volume I am currently working on), to pay close attention to those radical roots, even to draw on them for work that still needs to be done. So what I propose here is a paper attempting to explain the "mystery" of Oklahoma's progressive past and conservative present. Just one of the things I will use to explain the change over time is the recent book by Thomas Frank, *What's the Matter with Kansas? How Conservatives Won the Heart of America.* That book was actually the subject of Morgan's essay in the *Observer.* Why, Frank asks, do so many Americans in places such as Kansas— and Oklahoma!—vote against their economic interests? The basic answer seems to be their conservatism (on such issues as gun control, abortion, flag burning, gay marriage). I will conclude by suggesting that two starting points for reviving Oklahoma's progressive tradition are (1) becoming more aware of it historically and (2) organizing. And there's really no "mystery" about either one of those!

I was not just trying to be clever in tying into the "Mysterious Oklahoma" theme. Here is an excerpt from materials we were provided going into the festival: "'Mysterious': . . surprising, . . . baffling, . . . deep, . . . in process. . . . But writers seek to go deeper, to probe what is hidden, complex, changing, even what is at odds with prevailing views." My thinking about Oklahoma's political history fits well with much of that description! Indeed, the reason for my label "alternative views" is exactly because my goal is to present work "at odds with prevailing views."

But is the change from progressive past to conservative present a mystery? Some certainly think so. Walter Prescott Webb, in his classic 1930s volume *The Great Plains,* presented the area's persistent radicalism as one of the "Mysteries of the Great Plains." Last July at the Woody Guthrie Free Folk Festival in Guthrie's home town of Okemah, two members of the Green Party from California worked a booth next to the Woody Guthrie Coalition booth where I was working and constantly heard me explain my idea of "alternative views" to people; as the festival ended, they admitted to me that they had been shocked to learn that a conservative state such as Oklahoma had such progressive/radical elements in its past. And some years back a faculty colleague at East Central University saw Danney Goble's book, *Progressive Oklahoma*, lying on my desk. "Progressive Oklahoma," he said; "that's kind of an oxymoron, isn't it?" I saw what he meant, thought it was humorous, but also thought it was sad.

Part of my mission is to familiarize Oklahomans with their progressive past! Jenk Jones, of the Jones family that used to publish the *Tulsa Tribune*—a family hardly known for being on the left politically—recently devoted the first of his three lectures on Oklahoma's political history at the University of Oklahoma-Tulsa campus to "Our Radical Roots." One could even suggest that in the old days when someone referred to Oklahoma as a "red state," they might be referring to our red dirt, or Native American people (the name Oklahoma itself means "red man's land"), or, most relevant here, "reds," since Oklahoma had the strongest Socialist party in the country just before World War I. But now, of course, in the current red state/blue state terminology, Oklahoma is one of the reddest, being second only to Utah in terms of the degree of its conservative Republican voting habits.

I met a political scientist from the University of Oklahoma, Michael Givel, at that Woody Guthrie Festival last July. He bought my collection of "alternative views" of Oklahoma history, and kindly sent me a positive e-mail message about it. "Any idea why Oklahoma went from a hotbed of progressivism, populism, and socialism in the early days to its current reactionary state?" he asked. He went on: "I have read some things about the Green Corn Rebellion which apparently initiated the oppression and repression and destruction of the political left in Oklahoma." I replied that I did not have anything like a full answer to his question, so in his next message he went further. "My hypothesis," he said, "is that the destruction of the left was a planned effort by the Oklahoma Democratic Party, specifically but not exclusively in league with certain powerful corporate media moguls, other Oklahoma-specific corporate interests, and select religious leaders. Beneficiaries—direct or indirect—included certain fundamentalist congregations, and a small, wealthy elite, as Roxanne Dunbar-Ortiz has asserted, including oil and wheat interests."

Interesting, and thoughtful. Certainly it is true that populism, progressivism, and socialism were all present, some of them even strong, here in Oklahoma—as were, later, the civil rights movement, the anti-Vietnam War movement, and the anti-nuclear power movement. But I shared Givel's remarks with the historians I know at Rogers State University, where I now teach part-time—conservative Republicans all, which may be relevant here—and they suggested that Givel exaggerates the intentionality of the change, makes it sound almost conspiratorial, and also that he maybe overestimates just how progressive Oklahoma really was. It is true that Oklahoma has always been a mixed bag, so to speak. At the time of statehood in 1907, we were deeply influenced by the progressive reform ideas that were in the air nationally—but the first thing we did after becoming a state was to pass a set of Southern-style Jim Crow segregation laws. (Of course, the progressive movement itself was in some cases deeply flawed by its racism.) Even our Socialist party was a unique blend of socialism with Jeffersonian agrarianism and Christianity. (See Jim Bissett's *Agrarian Socialism in America: Marx, Jefferson, and Jesus in the Oklahoma Countryside, 1904-1920.*) So we have always had both—both progressive and conservative, both left and right. Even now, with Oklahoma being such a predictably conservative Republican state, substantial numbers of people do not fit that mold; red rectangular bumper stickers with a large blue dot have begun to appear around the state—the words read, "another bright blue dot in a really red state." Humorous perhaps, but also a powerful and important political statement.

Perhaps Thomas Frank can help us further in understanding the change in Oklahoma politics over the years by his insights about Kansas, which he chose because it is his home state; in some ways, he is talking about a national phenomenon. He writes of a great "backlash" since the 1960s, indeed in part a reaction against the movements of the 60s such as the women's movement, the anti-Vietnam War movement, the environmental movement, and the civil rights movement (perhaps especially the civil rights movement—race is close to the heart of Frank's analysis). Frank is not subtle. The backlash movement's "basic premise," he says, is that "culture outweighs economics as a matter of public concern—that Values Matter Most, as one backlash title has it. On those grounds it rallies citizens who would once have been reliable partisans of the New Deal to the standard of conservatism." But once the politicians who head this movement win election, Frank insists, "the only old-fashioned situation they care to revive is an economic regimen of low wages and lax regulations." Over the past three decades, he continues, they have "smashed the welfare state, reduced the tax burden on corporations and the wealthy, and generally facilitated the country's return to a nineteenth-century pattern of wealth distribution. Thus the primary contradiction of the backlash: it is a working-class movement that has done incalculable, historic harm to working-class people." Strong stuff. "The leaders of the backlash may talk Christ, but they walk corporate," Frank concludes. Sometimes, when he is writing about Kansas, one is tempted to simply insert "Oklahoma" instead, for much of his analysis seems to fit.

Roxanne Dunbar-Ortiz is also helpful in explaining the changes—nationally, and in Oklahoma. In the "Prologue" to the third and final installment in her excellent memoir series, *Blood on the Border: A Memoir of the Contra War,* she writes of a period of optimism for those on the left at the end of the Vietnam War. "The United States had been forced to abandon the Vietnam War, and the 1960s social and cultural revolution had pressured government officials into responding," she says. Yet, the "collapse of the mass movement" began to become apparent in the 1970s, in part due to "government policies and repression," but in part also due to the "movement's failure to establish long-term, broad-based coalitions"—a persistent theme in the history of the left. In Dunbar-Ortiz's view, this "sharp move to the Right both nationally and internationally" was consolidated in the election of Ronald Reagan in 1980. "The chilly wind of counterrevolution was upon us," she concludes. "The Cold War, US exceptionalism and unilateralism, crusader Christianity, laissez-faire capitalism, and anticommunism solidified into an iron fist."

But that progressive part of our past and present is still reality. Is it suggesting too much to say that a study of Oklahoma's progressive past can help to create more of those bright blue dots—not just bumper stickers, of course, but the substance that lies behind them? I have often heard it suggested, and perhaps you have also, that we study the past for the sake of the past, that historians should be totally objective. But the past does not have a "sake," does it? It is past. We study history to learn for today and to improve tomorrow. And historians, being human, cannot be totally objective, can they? In my experience, we should watch out for those who claim to be! For to the extent they succeed, they are doing history which tends to preserve the status quo—and it is difficult to imagine anything more unobjective, more political, than that! Instead, I want— influenced in part by Howard Zinn's approach in *A People's History of the United States*—to study/read/teach/write history in such a way as to contribute to the on-going struggle for peace and justice.

In the preface to my book, *"An Oklahoma I Had Never Seen Before,"* I wrote the following paragraph:

> In that inevitable taking of sides which comes from selection and emphasis in Oklahoma history, I prefer to try to tell the story of Oklahoma's prehistory from the point of view of the Spiro Mound people; of Indian removal from the viewpoint of the Cherokees; of the Civil War from the standpoint of the Seminole slaves; of the Run of '89 as seen by the Indians already here; of the coming of statehood as seen by the Sequoyah Convention; the First World War as seen by those who participated in the Green Corn Rebellion; the state's petroleum industry as seen by the workers in the fields; the coal mining industry as seen by the radical Italian labor organizer; the Ku Klux Klan as seen by the victims of the Tulsa Race Riot in 1921; the 1930s exodus as seen by the "Okies"; the state's "macho" image as seen by the victim of domestic violence or the gay individual; the state's failure to ratify the Equal Rights Amendment as seen by women; the University of Oklahoma's much-vaunted football success as seen by the bright students who feel compelled to leave the state for high-quality education and jobs, or as seen by the athlete who never gets a degree; and so on, to the limited extent that any one person, however he or she strains, can "see" history from the standpoint of others.

It seems important to me to try to do that kind of history. We should do it because it is *there*, because it is indeed part of the history of our great state. We should do it because the progressive, even radical, elements of our history are interesting, important, relevant, even inspiring. We should do it because the process will help to remove the "mystery" of our progressive past/conservative present—and perhaps give us a more progressive future.

CHAPTER 11

Woody Guthrie: Radical Okie Patriot

In 2012, I have had several opportunities that were exciting to me, in one case because of the Centennial of Woody Guthrie's birth, and in another because of the annual John Hope Franklin Symposium in Tulsa. What follows here is the lecture I gave at the Gilcrease Museum in Tulsa on February 3 to mark the opening of a major exhibition of Woody Guthrie materials. Since this volume is a "personal/historical" one, I have retained the lecture format and essentially reproduced the lecture as I gave it.

☮

Thank you.

I'm very excited and honored by this opportunity—as you'll see, Woody Guthrie means a great deal to me. But allow me to begin in a rather unusual manner, i.e., with a quote from someone else. This is from a pretty new book, published just last year, by Will Kaufman, entitled *Woody Guthrie: American Radical* . . . I think you'll see why I'm using it:

> When [Woody] Guthrie left his wife and children to seek a living for them all out west, he carried a part of Oklahoma with him: the prairie socialist tradition that his father had fought so hard to beat down, and which he himself would work to perpetuate. The radical struggle was inscribed into his very birthdate—July 14, 1912. While much has been made of the revolutionary overtones of the day—Bastille Day [in re the French Revolution]—it was the year of his birth that was the most significant. The year 1912 marked the near-zenith of the rising and falling tide of Oklahoma socialism, with the militant farmers giving Eugene

Debs and his Socialist Party over 16 percent of the state's vote in the national election (whereas the party could claim only 6 percent nationally). Socialism—the 'tempting serpent' with 'dangerous fangs,' as [Woody's Dad] Charley Guthrie described it—had thrown the state's Democrats 'into panic,' with the Socialists having increased their vote in every cotton-belt ballot since 1907. Debs had inflamed rural radicalism with his visions of a 'cooperative commonwealth' and the damnation of capitalism as 'inherently unjust, inhuman, unintelligent.' In Oklahoma the Socialist Party had championed the interests of 'agricultural workers' above all others, declaring them in official platforms the backbone of the state's 'working class; the Party's 'Renter's and Farmer's Program' promised to place control of the land in 'the hands of the actual tillers of the soil.' The Debsian party was populist in its appeal, St. George taking on the political dragon of "rent, credit, and taxes"—upon which the fortunes of all property entrepreneurs, Charley Guthrie included, were founded. The elder Guthrie could take little pleasure in the knowledge that it was his state—not New York— that was the epicenter of political radicalism in America.

But Woody could. (That little sentence is mine; in case it's not clear, the quote just ended.) Woody could. And some of us can also—at the very least, it should be noted that calling Oklahoma a "red state" once could have meant something very different from its conservative Republican status today. As Roxanne Dunbar-Ortiz wrote, eloquently and personally, in her essay "Growing Up Okie—and Radical" which appeared in my book *Alternative Oklahoma:*

First, there's the red soil in rural Canadian County, where I grew up, which my father tried to farm as a sharecropper and tenant. Second, Oklahoma originally was territory that the federal government established for the Indians who were forcibly removed from the Southeast region during the 1830s. My mother was in part descended from the 'Redman.' Third, my paternal grandfather was a Socialist and a Wobbly, active in the Socialist Party and the Industrial Workers of the World, and was driven out of Oklahoma in the 'Red Scare' of the Wilson administration. Not only my grandfather, but at least 20 percent of Oklahomans during that time were 'Reds.' That is where the irony comes in: Oklahoma has gone from 'Red' to 'red.'

(By the way, there's a new Socialist journal being published down in Norman called *Red State.*)

Woody also grew up Okie—and radical.

It's important, I think, before we go any further, to look at the meaning, or meanings, of the three words I used in my title: radical, Okie, and patriot.

First, the stereotypes. Radical is frequently associated with violence; I've had, many times over the years, students react against it....without having any real idea what it meant. Okie is frequently seen as a negative term, some low-life for respectable folks to look down on. And patriotism is usually seen as flag-waving, unquestioning support of whatever our politicians at the time lead us into, including war.

But now, the more accurate and helpful meanings....and then how they relate to Woody Guthrie.

Radical means "of or pertaining to root or origin . . . fundamental." Nothing about violence there. To be radical is to try to get to the root of a problem. And while it is certainly true that a "radical" on the political spectrum is someone who works to bring about fundamental changes in our political/economic/social system, to improve the quality of life for common folks, i.e., someone on the left, there is not, and has not been historically, any greater tendency on the part of radicals to use violence than people at other points on the political spectrum.

Okie, so often still in this state, has negative connotations. Perhaps most of all those come from the Joads in Steinbeck's *The Grapes of Wrath*. But I don't agree even with that. It always seemed to me that they were strong, determined, tough people, with a deep sense of connection to the land, and to family. (I'm thinking, among other things, of the scene in the movie where Grandpa Joad says "I ain't a goin' to Californy. This here's MY dirt," he says as he picks up a handful of it and lets it sift between his fingers; "It ain't no good, but it's mine." Part of the irony, of course, is that it *wasn't* really his, was it? The Joads, like so many others, were tenant farmers.)

Finally, the most fundamental meaning of patriotic is "of our fathers." To be a patriot, I suggest, is to feel connected to, to believe in deeply, the *ideals* on which this country was founded, spelled out best in the Declaration of Independence, such ideals as life and liberty and the pursuit of happiness and equality and self-determination that are so self-evident and inherent that no government has the right to take them away.

Now, to Woody.

Was he a radical? I'd say so, clearly. And you don't have to take my word for it....*Woody's* words, as usual, say it best. There are a couple of good stories that are relevant. One is that Woody was once told that he was considered too "left wing." After thinking about it a minute, he replied, in his best Okie drawl: "Ah, left wing, right wing, chicken wing....it don't make no difference to me....I just support programs that help my people." Indeed he did. Also, on one occasion when he was "accused" of being a Communist, he replied: "I ain't necessarily ever been a Communist, but I have been in the red most o' my life." Finally —of these stories that I think are great but can't necessarily be proven since we didn't have a tape recorder there at the time— Woody once said that the two people he admired most were Will Rogers and Jesus Christ. That's interesting to think about, among other reasons because Will is not usually regarded as being as radical as Woody (though there's some evidence that he was more so than his popular image suggests—he said something in 1931, for example, that feels pretty radical, and pretty relevant these days: "Ten men in our country could buy the world, and ten million can't buy enough to eat."). But it's also interesting because of Woody's mention of Jesus. As usual, again, Woody's words say it best, specifically his song lyrics. (Talking about music is kind of like talking about food, huh? But trust me, you don't want to hear me sing these....) Here are some of the lyrics for his song, "Jesus Christ:"

> Jesus Christ was a man who traveled through the land
> A hard-working man and brave
> He said to the rich, "Give your money to the poor,"
> And they laid Jesus Christ in his grave
>
> When Jesus come to town, all the working folks around
> Believed what He did say
> But the bankers and the preachers, they nailed Him on the cross,
> And they laid Jesus Christ in his grave
>
> And the people held their breath when they heard about His
> death
> Everybody wondered why

It was the big landlord and the soldiers that they hired
To nail Jesus Christ in the sky

This song was written in New York City
Of rich man, preacher, and slave
If Jesus was to preach what He preached in Galilee,
They would lay poor Jesus in His grave.

I can't resist one more, in the same vein....it was called "Christ for President," and it may feel even more relevant for today:

Let's have Christ our President
Let us have him for our king
Cast your vote for the Carpenter
That you call the Nazarene

The only way we can ever beat
These crooked politician men
Is to run the money changers out of the temple
And put the carpenter in

O it's Jesus Christ our President
God above our king
With a job and a pension for young and old
We will make hallelujah ring

Every year we waste enough
To feed the ones who starve
We build our civilization up
And we shoot it down with wars

But with the Carpenter in the seat
Way up in the Capital town
The USA would be on the way
Prosperity Bound!

I hope all that establishes pretty well that Woody was a radical—that just has to do, remember, with getting to the root of a problem, trying to improve the quality of life for common people.

Was Woody an Okie? No doubt. And I'd say a proud one. I'd also say that he spoke up more, and more effectively, for the folks who sometimes suffered from that label than anyone else did.

Finally, was Woody a patriot? Yes. But that means more than one thing. It does mean, in his case, that he believed, to a certain extent, in the cause of the US in World War II; he volunteered to serve in the Merchant Marine in that war. But it also means, especially if you put the two words "Okie" and "patriot" together, that he was deeply connected to the progressive/left/ liberal/RADICAL ideals of the early years of this state.

I've mentioned Will Kaufman's book, *Woody Guthrie: American Radical.* It's one of my favorites, because it does the best job of placing Woody in the best American radical tradition, where I think he clearly belongs. But I should also mention a few more. Both of the major biographies of Woody, by Joe Klein and Ed Cray, do a pretty good job of placing him in his Oklahoma context. So, to a certain extent, does the interestingly-titled study by Mark Allan Jackson: *Prophet Singer: The Voice and Vision of Woody Guthrie.*

But, not surprisingly, I want to draw to a great extent from my own two Oklahoma history books. For both have a strong Woody Guthrie connection. The first, *"An Oklahoma I Had Never Seen Before:" Alternative Views of Oklahoma History*, featured, at my insistence, a picture of the water towers in Woody's home town of Okemah on the cover. There are three of them, in case you haven't seen them. One says "HOT." One says "COLD" (and "OKEMAH"). And one says "HOME OF WOODY GUTHRIE." Needless to say, it was not without controversy when that last one was painted, in about 1970! And one of the essays featured in the book is by Harry Menig and carries the title, "Woody Guthrie: The Oklahoma Years, 1912-1929."

Menig insists that, though Woody spent only the first 17 years of his life in Okemah, in Oklahoma, that he was shaped forever by those years. Menig emphasizes that Woody's "contribution to American thought" was based on three ideals: [1] "The right of the common man to seek and maintain ownership of private property . . . Ideally expressed, this right would find culmination in a small self-sufficient farm." [2] "the sanctity of a strong family unit. . . He maintained that a strong family was a basic means of achieving social reform. The family unit would provide a sense of love and security, protecting the common man from the often inhumane corporate structures." And [3]: "Guthrie's third principle was directly inherited from his Oklahoma experience. With the end of the Okemah oil boom and the beginning of the catastrophic Dust Bowl and Great Depression, Guthrie witnessed the downfall of the common man. His belief in the right of every man to earn a living without fear or degradation served him as a guiding principle from the 1930s until his death in 1967." Concludes Menig: "The later works of Guthrie, when analyzed in terms of his three major beliefs, reveal that he never forsook his Oklahoma cultural heritage. [. . .] As America changed from an agricultural to an industrial society, Guthrie attempted to remind Americans that the agrarian love for a home, a family and a job were still worth preserving. Through the ballad tradition, Guthrie fought a battle against the creation of a society devoid of human compassion."

My second collection of what I like to call "alternative views" of Oklahoma history—because they emphasize women, minorities, common people, and radicals who worked to improve the quality of life for those common people, as well as looking at old, traditional topics in new ways, like an essay about the land run entitled "The Difficulty of Celebrating an Invasion" —my second one was called *Alternative Oklahoma: Contrarian Views of the Sooner State*, and was dedicated "To the memory and spirit of Woody Guthrie." It carried an essay by Thomas Conner, formerly with the *Tulsa World* and now with the *Chicago Sun-Times*, entitled "Getting Along: Woody Guthrie and Oklahoma's Red Dirt Musicians."

Conner's goal, as his title suggests, is to show Woody's continuing influence on Oklahoma music. And he does it well. Writing about the diverse musical sounds that are frequently lumped together under the "Red Dirt" label, Thomas suggests that what united them is "the influence . . . of a long-gone singer-songwriter and fellow Oklahoman: Woody Guthrie." Brandon Jenkins, one of the many songwriters influenced by Woody, says that "The way I'm most inspired by him is that when I write a song now, I try to keep the common man in mind . . . to speak for those people who can't speak for themselves." Somehow one of the stories Thomas tells that moves me most is the one about Doc James, the Caribbean-born leader of the Tulsa-based reggae band Local Hero. Thomas has just quoted Woody saying "A song tells you we're all the same color under our skin, and in a blood bank, the color is all the same." Then he quotes Doc James: "I heard about Woody a long time ago. I didn't know [then] he was from Oklahoma. I liked what he stood for as a musician and a person and a family man. Back in the day when he wrote songs about talking to the poorest man—that's a tradition in any culture all over the world. He did it, and he's legendary. Bob [Marley] did it. [Bob] Dylan did it. Speaking to the little man, making sure he's part of the conversation, keeping the people together on some level—that's what Woody was about . . . "

Thomas Conner doesn't quote this next item, but I can't resist; the words are Woody's, and they appear, along with his portrait, appropriately just to my left, on the wall above where I'm writing this at my computer:

> I hate a song that makes you think that you are not any good. I hate a song that makes you think that you are just born to lose. Bound to lose. No good to nobody. No good for nothing. Because you are too old or too young or too fat or too slim, too ugly or too this or too that. Songs that run you down or poke fun at you on account of your bad luck or hard traveling. I am out to fight those songs to my very last breath of air and my last drop of blood. I am out to sing songs that will prove to you that this is your world and that if it has hit you pretty hard and knocked you for a dozen loops, no matter what color, what size you are, how you are built, I am out to sing the songs that make you take pride in yourself and in your work. And the songs that I sing are made up for the most part by all sorts of folks just about like you. I could hire out to the other side, the big money side, and get several dollars every week just to quit singing my own kind of songs and to sing the kind that knock you down still farther and the ones that poke fun at you even more and the ones that make you think you've not got any sense at all. But I decided a long time ago that I'd starve to death before I'd sing any such songs as that. The radio waves and your movies and your jukeboxes and your song books are already loaded down and running over with such no good songs as that anyhow.

Thank you for that, Woody! And similarly, thank you for that sticker on your guitar that shows up in pictures so often, "This machine kills fascists," reminder of the power of music to help change things in a positive direction for common folks.

But I should get back briefly to Thomas Conner's essay. Thomas also emphasizes Woody's deep connection to

Oklahoma. He does so in part by quoting other people on the subject, including Guy Logsdon (who I am personally convinced knows as much about Woody as anyone alive—and who does a pretty mean Woody tune now and then also): "The unifying theme in Woody's music is that he wrote about the land he loved. He played the melodies and music that came from the land he loved, from Oklahoma, one of the most culturally diverse places in America." And including Nora Guthrie, Woody's daughter: "Everything he did and fought for had to do with the basic values he learned in Oklahoma. When I lecture in Oklahoma, I tell people, 'You think he's talking about other people's rights and other people's problems, but he was talking about your grandfather ... These were his people. Everything he wrote, especially the early songs, was about your family.' He wasn't that expanded back then. What did he know from America? All he knew was that someone's grandmother lost the farm or someone's cousin was done wrong. Everything he cared about came from his love for Oklahoma ... When he finally traveled to other places, he found that they were having the same problems, so he could become this spokesperson for America . . . "

So Woody felt this deep sense of connection to Oklahoma. But it took Oklahoma a while to get around to honoring him. I've mentioned his name on the water tower in his home town of Okemah—requests from the city council to have it removed continued as late as 1988, when one councilman made a motion to replace it with an American flag....the motion, however, died for lack of a second. Thomas Conner suggests it was that very year that the anti-Woody sentiment in Okemah and throughout the state began to wane. And this summer, if you can stand the heat, you can attend the 15th annual Woody Guthrie Festival in Okemah, July 11-15....including, obviously, what would have been Woody's 100th birthday, July 14th.

Outside Okemah, around Oklahoma, other interesting things have happened, are happening. I believe it was in 2004 that Charles Banks Wilson's wonderful portrait of Woody was hung in the state capitol in Oklahoma City. As Woody's son, Arlo, said at that summer's Woodyfest in Okemah, "Damn, they finally hung Daddy in Oklahoma City!" Of course, Arlo has a delightful sense of humor, and a story-telling style not unlike his father. He's been known in recent years to support the idea of moving the festival to the fall because of the intense heat and humidity in Okemah in July. Woody died, you see, in 1967, on October 3. So Arlo said, basically: Those of us who loved Daddy, and love his music, could come together and celebrate, like we do now. And those who hated Daddy and his music could come together and celebrate his death. And we could all be a lot cooler while doing it.

Woody's song, "Oklahoma Hills," has been our official state folk song for some ten years now. Fred Harris—one-time prominent Oklahoma Democratic politician who moved on to the US Senate and sought the Democratic Presidential nomination in both 1972 and 1976—has suggested, somewhat facetiously, I think, that Woody's "This Land Is Your Land" should be the national anthem. Let me tell the story: Arlo was doing a fund-raiser for Fred's Presidential campaign at the Cain's Ballroom here in Tulsa in 1976. I was seated, as I remember it, between my wife, Carole, and Fred. Arlo had us all stand while he led us in a sing-along of "This Land"—including the sometimes-forgotten verses, of which more in a moment—and as we finished, Fred poked me with his elbow and said, "That song ought to be the national anthem!"

"This Land Is Your Land," you see, has often been seen as a celebration of the beauty of the American landscape. And it is that. But it's not *just* that. Arlo remembers vividly the day his father took him out in the back yard, after his Huntington's Disease had advanced to the point that it was very hard for him to play his guitar at all, to teach him the words, *all* the words, to the song; he was apparently already concerned that some of the verses were frequently being left out. Here are the words:

> *Chorus*
> This land is your land, this land is my land
> From California to the New York Island
> From the redwood forest to the gulf stream waters
> This land was made for you and me
>
> As I was walking a ribbon of highway
> I saw above me an endless skyway
> I saw below me a golden valley

This land was made for you and me (repeat chorus)

I've roamed and rambled and I've followed my footsteps
To the sparkling sands of her diamond deserts
And all around me a voice was sounding
This land was made for you and me (repeat chorus)

The sun came shining as I was strolling
The wheat fields waving and the dust clouds rolling
The fog was lifting, a voice came chanting
This land was made for you and me (repeat chorus)

Was a great high wall there that tried to stop me
A sign was painted said "Private Property"
But on the other side, it didn't say nothin'
That side was made for you and me (repeat chorus)

One bright Sunday morning in the shadow of the steeple
By the relief office I saw my people
As they stood hungry, I stood there wondering if
This land was made for you and me (repeat chorus)

Nobody living can ever stop me
As I go walking my freedom highway
Nobody living can make me turn back
This land was made for you and me (repeat chorus)

Allow me just a brief side story, about that song, but also about Woody's influence, not just in Oklahoma and around the country, but also around the world. It was the mid 1990s. I was teaching at a university in Hungary. I was asked to give a lecture about something distinctive/representative of where I was from. I chose to talk about Woody Guthrie. And when one of my students, Zoltan Siklosi, found out about that, he very excitedly offered to play the song for the occasion. I said, "You know Woody Guthrie's 'This Land Is Your Land'?" "Oh, yes," he answered, "including the verses you Americans so often leave out!" So Zoltan led us in a sing-along. I love singing along on that song. But that occasion was one of my favorites. Needless to say, Carole and I were the only Okies in the crowd, indeed I think the only Americans in the crowd, which gave it a different feel.

In 2006, Woody Guthrie was finally inducted into the Oklahoma Hall of Fame. I like to think that the persistent nominations of him for that honor by Thomas Conner, Guy Logsdon, and myself had something to do with it. In my nomination letter in 2005, I quoted the criteria: inductees "must have made a major national or international impact through their accomplishments and contributions." And then I said, "It seems absolutely clear to me that Woody Guthrie qualifies!" I noted, among other things, that he had already been inducted into both the Country Music Hall of Fame and the Rock and Roll Hall of Fame (as an "Early Influence"). In any case, whether I helped or not, Woody was inducted in 2006.

And now, this year, the centennial year of Woody's birth, somehow appropriately, Woody is coming home to Oklahoma. I'm thinking of recent news items in the *Tulsa World* such as "Woody Guthrie Archives: Moving to Tulsa . . . An Icon's Return" (December 28, 2011) and "State warming to native son . . . Events to mark Guthrie's centennial and a new Tulsa center erode doubts," (January 1, 2012), both by Wayne Greene. Local events include the move of the Woody Guthrie Archives to a new center here in Tulsa, with the help of the George Kaiser Family Foundation....Woody coming home!; a star-studded concert at the Brady Theater featuring Arlo Guthrie, John Cougar Mellencamp, and others; an academic conference at the University of Tulsa on March 10 entitled "Different Shades of Red: Woody Guthrie and the Oklahoma Experience" and featuring, among others, Will Kaufman, Thomas Conner, Guy Logsdon, and Hugh Foley of Rogers State University—other, similar, conferences will occur later all around the country, and to a certain extent all around the world; *and* the opening of the exhibit here at Gilcrease.

So, in conclusion: I'm a historian; I know better than to romanticize individuals from history. I don't want to do that with Woody Guthrie. He was imperfect. Aren't we all? Isn't that just a way of saying that we're human? But, Woody Guthrie: radical, Okie, patriot. "From My Point of View" [my lecture was part of a series using that title], we could use him today! As Steve Earle sang, "Come back, Woody Guthrie, come back to us now, Tear your eyes from paradise and rise again somehow." But that's not likely, is it? So let's just learn what we can from him. I hope this lecture will help a bit with that process; I'm convinced the exhibit opening here at Gilcrease, and the many other events going on in this centennial year of his birth, will help as well.

CHAPTER 12

The Personal Politics of Reconciliation

Most readers of this volume are well aware by now that I don't think much in terms of heroes/heroines when I do history. But it's not too much to call Woody Guthrie, in the previous chapter, and John Hope Franklin, in this chapter, heroes of mine. As a proud Okie myself, I'm very proud that they both came from our state. They are very different, of course, Guthrie one of America's great folk musicians, Franklin one of America's great historians. The symposium that honors Franklin in Tulsa each year is an amazing and important event, in my opinion; I was honored to be a part of it. The theme of the symposium for 2012 was "The Politics of Reconciliation." My lecture follows— again, like the Woody Guthrie essay in the previous chapter, as given. It's my hope that this call for a personal politics of reconciliation provides an appropriate conclusion for a collection of "personal/historical" essays.

☮

Howard Zinn, as many of you probably know, was best known for his 1980 *magnum opus*, the two million[+] best seller *A People's History of the United States*. And certainly I respect that work greatly, was much influenced by it in my own approach to history, including Oklahoma history. For people unfamiliar with it, I like to explain briefly that by "people's history" Zinn meant history "from the bottom up" or "from the outside in." He did *not* focus, in other words, on Presidents, kings and queens, generals, and the rich, as so much history traditionally had done.

He focused, rather, on common folks, and always looked at history from the point of view of those on the bottom of the social/economic/political spectrum rather than the top, and from the point of view of those on the outside of the power structure rather than the inside. His heros and heroines were those who worked for change, to improve the quality of life for the people. I don't know about you, but in Oklahoma history, with all due respect, I'm not much interested in governors and oil millionaires—I can't relate to them. I'm more interested in the voters—and non-voters—the workers in the oil fields, women, minorities, common folks, and those radicals/progressives/reformers/liberals who worked to improve the quality of their lives.

But, I bring up Howard Zinn today to make a particular point, related, I think you'll see, to the theme of this symposium, the politics of reconciliation, and to the theme of my paper, the *personal* politics of reconciliation. The two books of Zinn's that I want to use are not nearly so well known as his *People's History*. Both appeared in 1964: one he called *The Southern Mystique* and the other, on the important Student Nonviolent Coordinating Committee and his work with them as a faculty adviser, was entitled *SNCC: The New Abolitionists*. (Interesting title, don't you think, comparing those young people, white and black, with the abolitionists who fought over a hundred years earlier to rid our country of the evil of human slavery?)

The Southern Mystique—also an interesting title—was essentially an interpretive essay on the South and its history and culture. Zinn dedicated it, significantly, "To my students at Spelman College and the student movement in Atlanta, without whom this book could not have been written." Which finally gets me to the point that I wanted to start with....but I felt it was necessary to give that bit of background. "Perhaps the most striking development in the South," Zinn wrote, "is not that the process of desegregation is under way but that the mystique with which Americans have always surrounded the South is beginning to vanish." There existed, Zinn believed, "a strange and damnable unanimity among segregationists, white liberals, and Negroes on one fervent belief": "the mystery of *negritude*—the irreducible kernel, after all sociological peelings, of race difference." But, and here is the key, in my opinion, the reason I chose as my title for this presentation the *personal* politics of reconciliation: There is, insists Zinn, "a magical and omnipotent dispeller of the mystery," and that is simply *contact*. "Contact—" he wrote, "but it must be massive, unlike those 'integrated' situations in the North, and it must be equal, thus excluding maid-lady relationships of the South—[contact] destroys the man-made link between physical difference and behavior." For race consciousness, Zinn insisted, is hollow: "its formidable-looking exterior is membrane-thin and is worn away by simple acts of touch, the touching of human beings in contact that is massive, equal, and prolonged."

Zinn's optimism always impressed me; you don't have to get to know his work very well to realize that it was one of his persistent characteristics. He spoke highly of famous historian C. Vann Woodward's pioneering work *The Strange Career of Jim Crow*, published originally in 1955, feeling that it was the most forceful historical attack on the notion that the South's racial mores were unchangeable. Zinn acknowledged that he was being optimistic, "insistently optimistic." What he called for was *integration*, not just *desegregation*, explaining that "You have desegregation when the legal bars to racial contact are lifted. You have integration when that contact actually takes place." He felt lucky, he said, to have had the opportunity to work and live over a period of years with his wife and family in a predominantly black community. "This kind of total immersion is not just educational, in the pallid sense of book learning; it is transforming, as real education should be." "Living together, working together, bring the fastest results in destroying race prejudice," he believed, based on his own experience.

When I was talking about this paper with my friend Charles Angeletti, he insisted that Zinn's very decision to accept the job at Spelman, a school for African American women in Atlanta, showed that he personally/innately believed in the *personal* politics of reconciliation; Zinn was, after all, the child of a poor Jewish immigrant family in New York City, and had never even been south before. He certainly did some things right there, didn't he? One of his students at Spelman, Pulitzer Prize-winning African American novelist (*The Color Purple*) Alice Walker, wrote these words in a promotional blurb for Zinn's 1994 book *You Can't Be Neutral On A Moving Train*: "What can I say that will in any way convey the love, respect, and admiration I feel for this unassuming hero who was my teacher and mentor, this radical historian and people-loving 'trouble-maker,' this man who stood with us and suffered with us? Howard Zinn was the best teacher I ever had, and the funniest. Here is a history and a history maker to give us hope; especially the young to whom he has always committed so much of his life."

Zinn's other 1964 book, on SNCC, was quite different from *The Southern Mystique*, of course, but agreed on the basic point about contact. In response to the question about whether white people and black people can truly live together as friends in the United States, Zinn's answer, based on SNCC and his experience with those young people, was a cautious but powerful "yes." "Never in the history of the United States has there been a movement where the lives, day by day, of Negro and white people are so entwined physically, intellectually, emotionally," he wrote. He acknowledged that it had not always gone smoothly, that it was easier for the young than for the old, that there was no single correct path toward putting race behind us, and that it was easier to note some common mistakes. It is a mistake, for example, to think that one can forget completely about race—but also a mistake not to try. It's also clearly a mistake "for a white person to play at being black," or to "romanticize the Negro, simply because in this period of our history, *he* is carrying the torch of American idealism." But, just like in *The Southern Mystique*, Zinn insisted again here that "the key to a solution of the dilemma is contact—continued and massive contact among people of different races."

My experience—relevant here, I hope, because my subject, after all, is the *personal* politics of reconciliation—tells me that Howard Zinn was correct. You see, I was born and raised in the small town of Greenwood, Sebastian County, Arkansas, over by Ft. Smith. I was born in 1940, so I grew up there in the 40s and 50s. I love the small towns of the South, like Greenwood. I love the smallness, the friendliness, the neighborliness, the food, the family focus, the values, the whole culture. Well, *almost* the whole culture. I never liked the gossip much, but it does seem to be part of the package, doesn't it? But my point here is *racism*. I grew up with a lot of it. I heard the n-word a lot in Greenwood. But I never heard it from my Mother! Indeed, I remember one occasion when I came home from school upset about what kids were saying about the Rev. Dr. Martin Luther King, Jr. —"Communist," "trouble-making *n*....," etc. I talked to Mama about it, and two things stand out in my memory. First, she said "Davie, we have to listen to that man, you know—he's a Baptist preacher." It meant a lot to me then, and somehow means even more to me now, that even as King led the civil rights movement that was shaking the very foundation of the social order of the South, including Greenwood, Mom was able to see the good. The other thing that stands out in my memory is how the conversation ended: With a Motherly wag of the finger, she said "You'd better not ever let me hear of *you* calling him names like that!"

So when I left Greenwood to start college at Eastern New Mexico University, in Portales, in the fall of 1958, and for the first time in my life was exposed to diversity—including Native Americans, Hispanic Americans, African Americans—I was not totally unprepared, thanks in large part to Mom. There was a fellow freshman named Robert, African American, who was in two classes with me that fall, and as I look back on it now, I'd say Robert above all others—though there were others—helped me begin to see the truth in Howard Zinn's claim in *The Southern Mystique* that "a Negro *known* [This was written in 1964, remember when "Negro" was perfectly acceptable usage.] is a person with dozens of different characteristics, one of the least important of which is blackness."

By Christmas-time that first year, Robert and I had developed enough of a friendship that we decided to share transportation home for the holidays. What that meant, since I had a car and he didn't, was that he would ride with me from Portales to Greenwood, then catch a bus the rest of the way home to Gadsden, Alabama. It would be more fun, we figured, he could help with the driving, and with the gas—after all, it was costing like 20 cents a gallon at the time. We got to Shamrock, Texas, and I was getting hungry and started waxing eloquent about a little restaurant I was familiar with there. I remember thinking Robert wasn't responding very positively, and couldn't think why. When we got close enough to see it, I said "There it is, up there on the right," and Robert blurted out "I don't want to go there, Davie. They probably wouldn't serve me, they might not serve you if you're with me. Couldn't we go someplace else?" We drove on up the road to a drive-in, where we ate in the car together, and I was sensitized enough by then to notice that we got some pretty unfriendly looks even there. That little incident was a turning point for me. I remember feeling embarrassment at my naiveté, and *rage* that my friend Robert and I couldn't sit down together and eat a hamburger where we wanted to.

Suffice it to say that by the time I arrived at the University of Oklahoma in the fall of 1963 to begin work on my Ph.D. in history I was participating actively, if in small ways, in the civil rights movement.

But first, allow me to share a little story about an incident that occurred just the other day, as I write this, and that served as my most recent reminder of the fundamental sameness of we humans. I was in the Dollar General store in Langley, six miles away from Spavinaw where we live, buying napkins of a particular type that are my wife Carole's favorite. The woman at the register was friendly, and commented about the napkins, so I said something like "Yes, they're my wife's favorites, and after 37 years, you learn how to score a few brownie points." As I completed the transaction and headed toward the door, a black gentleman standing there said "That would be 1975, right?" Obviously, he had overheard the conversation and was referring to the date of our marriage. Somewhat taken aback, I said "Yes, why?" Turned out, that's when he and his wife were married also. He asked our anniversary date, and I told him September 26. When I asked theirs, he said June 19. I said "Wow, that's my birthday." Which led to a shift in the conversation to the African American celebration of "Juneteenth." He was impressed with my knowledge of that, and I told him it was largely because I was a retired history prof. He was from Denver, by the way, his wife from nearby Vinita, Oklahoma, and he even knew of my friend Charles Angeletti at Metropolitan State University of Denver who I mentioned earlier. By then, it was time to go our separate ways. But what a fun incident; I love that kind of thing, that kind of friendliness, that kind of connection. We shook hands and moved on, and I would argue that the color of our skin made no difference—here's a nice friendly guy who got married the same year I did.

But, pardon that diversion: on to graduate school at OU. One of the new friends I made that fall of '63 was Jimmie Lewis Franklin, and we are still friends today. How many friends do you have who've been your friend for 50 years? Back in the 60s, we cried on each other's shoulders about the travails of getting a Ph.D.; today we cry on each other's shoulders about the travails of growing old. Jimmie became only the second African American to receive a Ph.D. from the University of Oklahoma, and went on to a distinguished career, including the presidency of the Southern Historical Association, a professorship at Vanderbilt University, and three books on Oklahoma history with which some of you might be familiar: *Born Sober: Prohibition in Oklahoma, 1907-1959*, *The Blacks in Oklahoma* (a volume in the Newcomers to a New Land Series), and the more extensive *Journey Toward Hope: A History of Blacks in Oklahoma*. Jimmie also contributed chapters to both of my Oklahoma history books, one on blacks and sense of place in Oklahoma, the other on blacks and the quest for freedom here. Recently, my friendship with Jimmie ramped up a notch, so to speak, when I asked him to write a foreword for a forthcoming book of mine [obviously, that's *this* book]; to get back to the 60s, allow me to quote from that: "In 1965, a hate-filled citizen of Selma, Alabama, clubbed to death a minister named James Reeb who had gone South to participate in the Selma to Montgomery March for voting rights. Students at the University of Oklahoma held a memorial service for Reeb as a small group of racially conservative students looked on in protest, one of whom aggressively waved a small confederate flag. Davis Joyce attended that celebration of Reverend Reeb's life; and the fact that he chose to do that with the writer of this foreword—an African-American native of Mississippi—said much about influences upon him before he came to the University at Norman." Jimmie and I, and our wives, are part of a group of five couples who get together every year or so in what we call an "OU History Ph.D. Reunion." Five old men who received our Ph.D. in either 1967 or 1968, and our wives, sitting around telling stories about old times—some of which are actually true! It'll be in Las Vegas, "Sin City," this year, because that's where the Franklins have retired, but I doubt there'll be much sinning going on.

Two other individuals I want to mention briefly, along with their work, are Hannibal Johnson and Eddie Faye Gates.

Hannibal and I have developed a bit of a friendship in the last few years, I dare say. We met at events like the Red Dirt Book Festival in Shawnee, when we noticed we were interested in each other's programs and when we were seated next to each other at a couple of book signing events . . . Johnson, Joyce. Now we get together occasionally for lunch or coffee. I like and respect Hannibal very much, including his writings. I've read all his books, including those on the Greenwood district and Oklahoma's all-black towns. As he noted when he signed one of his books for me, "We're like-minded as regards the importance of what I've called parallel historical narratives." But the book of Hannibal's that I think illustrates our connection best is the one called *Mama Used to Say: Wit and Wisdom from the Heart and Soul.* Hannibal and I have laughed about how much an old white guy and a much-younger black guy who both have roots in western Arkansas share. This book illustrates that best! In his Prologue, Hannibal wrote, "I owe much of my modest success to the thoughtful guidance and wise counsel of my mother." So do I. "This tribute features a sampling of Mama's remarkable lessons, through precept and example, on navigating the ebb and flow of life's ever-shifting waters," Hannibal wrote, and concludes, "May the pages that follow stimulate your mind, warm your heart, and soothe your soul." They did all that for me. I swear I could have written some of the material in the book about my own Mother. Hannibal is aware of the universality of what he does in this wonderful little book. "Mothers around the world lovingly pass

along to their children timeless expressions, sage advice, and
bedrock values," he notes. One other thing I should mention
about Hannibal is his important work here, for the John Hope
Franklin Center for Reconciliation, and specifically for this
symposium. He also made an important contribution on the
subject of reparations for the 1921 riot here in the most recent
issue of *Oklahoma Humanities*. (The entire issue was devoted to the
theme of reconciliation.)

Eddie Faye Gates was a student of mine many years ago at
the University of Tulsa, and was kind enough to mention me in
one of her books, *Miz Lucy's Cookies*, indeed to call me one of her
"favorite professors." She also had one of our children as her
student. A couple of her other books, for those of you unfamiliar
with her work, are *They Came Searching: How Blacks Sought the
Promised Land in Tulsa*, and *Riot on Greenwood: The Total Destruction of
Black Wall Street*. I should note that she also served on the Tulsa
Race Riot Commission.

After having my proposal approved for this symposium, I
read a book which I got for a Christmas present entitled *Prophetic
Encounters: Religion and the American Radical Tradition*, by Dan
McKanan. Parts of it feel relevant to me here. McKanan refers,
for example, to the "transformative encounters with black
friends" experienced by the white abolitionist Grimke sisters of
South Carolina, and quotes Angelina Grimke specifically
addressing black women in 1838, saying "it is only by associating
with you that we shall be able to overcome" white prejudice.
Harriet Beecher Stowe of *Uncle Tom's Cabin* fame "assumed that
personal encounters between blacks and whites would translate
into common action against slavery." Jane Addams of Hull
House fame is quoted insisting that "the things which make men
alike are finer and better than the things that keep them apart." I
could go on, but let me mention just one more, from a more
recent era. McKanan insists that CORE (the Congress of Racial
Equality) "revived the one-on-one practices of interracial
encounter that had defined the abolitionist era," and
furthermore that "For the interracial teams that took CORE's
message on the road, integration was an end in itself and not
merely a means to African American empowerment. Because

they insisted on a harmony between means and ends, they proudly called themselves the Congress *of*—not merely *on*—Racial Equality."

I want to move toward my conclusion by talking a bit about John Hope Franklin himself. Most of you don't need me to remind you of the basics: Born in Rentiesville, one of Oklahoma's all-black towns, he was the son of Buck Colbert Franklin, the lawyer here in Tulsa who did so much important legal work following the 1921 race riot. Franklin himself went on to become, in my opinion and that of many others, one of the most important American historians of the twentieth century. He wrote many books, but his best known is surely *From Slavery to Freedom: A History of Negro Americans*, originally published in 1947. At the time of publication of Franklin's autobiography, *Mirror to America*, in 2005, it was claimed that *From Slavery to Freedom* had sold over 3.5 million copies. It is now available in a 9th edition, co-authored with Evelyn Brooks Higginbotham and published in 2010. Ninth edition—did you catch that? A book doesn't go through that many editions unless it is important and/or doing well. The sub-title, by the way, is now "a history of African Americans," reflecting changing usage over the years. I used the edition that was current as of 1969-1970 when I first taught black history at the University of Tulsa that year.

Before continuing with Franklin, a few words about that teaching experience. My colleague Michael Whalon and I team-taught it; perhaps needless to say, it was the first time black history was offered at TU, and it filled up. But Mike and I were both white. We had only one black student take the course. In a "personal reaction" paper we had students write at the end of the semester, she said something which meant a great deal to me, essentially: I came into this course with considerable misgivings —what could a couple of white TU profs teach me about my history? I came out of it having learned a lot, and realizing that history is history, no matter who teaches it. I've mentioned my friend Charles Angeletti. We grew up together in Arkansas, and he too "pioneered" black history where he was teaching, Metropolitan State University of Denver—two white boys from Greenwood teaching black history. We found that unusual enough, and certainly a powerful enough experience for both of us, that many years ago we did a presentation on it together at a meeting of the National Social Science Association. Charles, though, has had an experience I have not: team-teaching with a black colleague in the Criminal Justice department, Richard Jackson. Together, they presented a program at the most recent meeting of the NSSA entitled "The Transformative Nature of Interracial Team Teaching." Transformative.

I have inserted in my copy of Franklin's *Mirror to America* a program from the Annie Henry Club of Christ's Temple Christian Methodist Episcopal Church's annual observance of Negro History Week in 1970, and, I'm proud to say, I have Franklin's autograph on it. Which leads me, consistent with the theme of my paper, to a few personal remarks about John Hope Franklin. I'm very pleased that I had the opportunity to get to know him a bit. I don't want to exaggerate—we were not really friends. But think about this: I'm a new, young, unknown assistant professor of history at TU in those days, while Franklin is already one of the major names in the profession. But I would see him at events, like that Negro History Week program, or at a meeting of the Southern Historical Association in Memphis, and he would know me. I remember on one such occasion, when we had not seen each other for a few years, he was embarrassed because he couldn't think of my name, and said something like, "Oh, you're that young man from Tulsa!" In short, I'm convinced that John Hope Franklin was not only a great historian, but also a very nice person. I've learned much from reading his books, and I'm also honored to have known him. It feels really good to me that he is being honored here in his home state, that this Center/Symposium are named for him, and that his portrait now hangs in the state capital.

I started this paper by dealing with Howard Zinn. Are you aware that Zinn and Franklin died close to the same time? Along with Ivan Van Sertima, known especially for his work insisting on important African contributions to global culture. William Loren Katz wrote about that on his web site, referring to all three as "friends," and saying that they each "challenged aspects of the cheerfully-bigoted narrative that has passed for history in schools, colleges, texts and the media," and further that "the books of these innovative scholars amounted to a vast underground railroad of treacherous knowledge." Of Franklin specifically, Katz said: He "wrote in a time when Henry Steele Commager and Samuel Eliot Morison, Pulitzer Prize historians, used their widely-used college text, *The Growth of the American Republic*, to describe slavery in this hideous way: 'As for Sambo, . . . he suffered less than any other class in the South from its peculiar institution.' Franklin faced a citizenry schooled on notions that people of African descent really benefitted from slavery and had no history worth recounting. His response was to painstakingly detail how people of African descent contributed substantially to each stage of America's economic and democratic growth." Indeed he did.

And one of the things he helped me to understand is that politics is personal. In this paper, I've tried to combine the two. And I make no apology for that, for I have come to the firm belief that we compartmentalize parts of our lives too much, especially trying to separate the personal out from the professional....and the political. So when I hear racist language, and somehow even more when I hear racist jokes, I take it personal. I think of the couple in their 80s I have gotten to know the last few years hanging out in Frosty and Edna's Café up in Langley. They are white. But they've taken in, for some period of time, some 100 foster children over the years. And when we were talking about it one time, I remember her poking me on the hand with her finger for emphasis and saying "Perfesser [she can't get my name right], it don't make no difference what color a kid's skin is when they need help," etc. They have helped Anglo American, Native American, Hispanic American, and African American. So again, I take racist language personally. I think of John Hope Franklin. I think of Jimmie Franklin. I think of Hannibal Johnson, Eddie Faye Gates, my friend Robert from back in the 50s. I think of the black folks at the Tulsa Teachers Credit Union's North Pointe branch, where we bank, the growing number of black members of our church, All Souls Unitarian.

I take it personally.

So I believe that reconciliation is/must be deeply personal. We need to reach out across the artificial boundaries that we allow to divide us—such artificial boundaries as nationality, religion . . . and race. On race, the Rev. Dr. Martin Luther King, Jr., said it best, as he did so many things: We must learn to judge people *not* "by the color of their skin, but by the content of their character." When we do, I believe, it will help us to communicate more effectively and in a more civil manner in this day of deep polarization in our society, our culture . . . our politics. When we reach this realization of the significant degree to which politics is personal, it might even contribute to our being able to come together to help our nation live up to its promise. In any case, shouldn't we at least try? The personal politics of reconciliation.

Thank you.

Author photo taken just north of Spavinaw,
south of the T General Store.

Davis D. Joyce was born near Greenwood, Arkansas, in the area soon to become Fort Chaffee, in June of 1940. After graduating high school at Greenwood in 1958, he moved to Clovis, New Mexico, because of asthma-type problems, to live temporarily with his Uncle D. W. and Aunt Geneva Joyce, and attended Eastern New Mexico University in nearby Portales, where he majored in music for two years, then changed to history, and graduated in 1961. For his M. A. in history, he attended New Mexico State University, graduating in 1963. And for the Ph. D., he moved to Norman, Oklahoma, securing the degree in 1968.

Joyce had already started teaching at the University of Tulsa in 1966. In the meantime, he had begun to consider Oklahoma his home, and still does. The other university where he spent a substantial period of his teaching career was East Central University in Ada, from the 1980s until his retirement from full-time teaching in 2002, when East Central honored him with Professor Emeritus of History status. He also taught one semester at the University of Keele in England, and two years at the University of Debrecen in Hungary; while in Hungary, he co-authored a textbook with his colleague and friend Tibor Glant entitled *United States History: A Brief Introduction for Hungarian Students*, which is still in use at Debrecen and other universities. Since retirement, he has taught part-time at Rogers State University in Claremore.

Joyce has been the author, co-author, or editor of ten books to this point, including *Howard Zinn: A Radical American Vision*, *Edward Channing and the Great Work*, *The Writing of American History* (co-author with Michael Kraus), *"An Oklahoma I Had Never Seen Before:" Alternative Views of Oklahoma History*, and *Alternative Oklahoma: Contrarian Views of the Sooner State*.

Joyce and his wife, Carole, are now retired to a cottage near Lake Spavinaw, in northeastern Oklahoma.

www.ingramcontent.com/pod-product-compliance
Lightning Source LLC
Chambersburg PA
CBHW062059080426
42734CB00012B/2698